RUSTIC

TRADITIONS

RUSTIC TRADITIONS

RALPH KYLLOE

GIBBS·SMITH PUBLISHER

SALT LAKE CITY

ABOUT THE AUTHOR

RALPH KYLLOE, Ed.D., a professor at Tufts University, is recognized as a leading authority on rustic furniture. His personal collection has been exhibited at museums in New York and Boston. He runs an antique and decorating business in the Lake George region of the Adirondacks and New Hampshire. Feature articles about Ralph Kylloe have appeared in publications such as *Country Living, Architectural Digest,* and *Traditional Homes.* He has published two books and numerous articles on Indiana Hickory furniture and recently received the distinguished Cleo Grant from the Indiana Historical Society for continued work research on the subject.

First paperback edition 1995

97 96 95   5 4 3 2 1

Copyright © 1993 by Ralph Kylloe

Photographs © 1993 by Ralph Kylloe unless other wise noted.

This is a Peregrine Smith Book,

published by

Gibbs Smith, Publisher

P.O. Box 667

Layton, Utah 84041

Design by Traci O'Very Covey

Printed in Hong Kong

Library of Congress Cataloging-in-Publication Data

Kylloe, Ralph R.

    Rustic traditions/Ralph Kylloe.

      p. cm.

    ISBN 0-87905-670-3 (pbk.)

    1. Country furniture--United States. I. Title.

NK2405.K96 1993

749.213--dc20   93-14068

                      CIP

DEDICATION

For my mother, Elizabeth Ann. Thanks for the years of tolerance, patience, and guidance.

C O N T E N T S

PREFACE

I started out as an academic but ended up in the antique and decoration business. I fell in love with rustic furniture and the thrill of the "treasure hunt." I have had the pleasure of finding and owning many of the pieces pictured in this book.

Because of my background, I wanted to know more about a piece than just what it was worth. Rustic furniture is a significant part of our heritage, so not only the pieces but also the history behind them needs to be documented and preserved.

Most of the furniture and accessories shown here are antique. Many of the pieces are in private collections and have not been published before. Throughout the book, I have tried to add personal notes on the history of the maker or the piece. Significantly more information is available but could not be included here.

Another aim of the book is to depict the settings in which the pieces are being used today. Many of these pieces have not moved from their locations in years and years. They are still being used in much the same way they were originally. Most of the scenes in the book were photographed as they are, and little or no attempt was made to manipulate the surroundings. The locations of the pieces and the names of their owners are not included to protect their privacy.

During the past few years, I have been fortunate to have had many pieces in my own collection featured in museums and on the pages of magazines. Needless to say, it has been quite thrilling to receive a phone call from an individual and be told that his or her grandfather made a certain piece. So it was with Reverend Ben Davis's items. Davis was the quintessential rustic builder of the South, and I was lucky enough to speak directly with the grandson with whom he lived for many years. This kind of connection has happened on several other occasions.

Another exciting thing has been to walk into a place that has been shut up for seventy years and see treasures that have long been forgotten. It is like taking a step back into history.

I must also say that I am very impressed with the owners of many of the pieces in this book. One person in Georgia, with whom I spoke only briefly on the phone, gave me permission to visit his summer cottage to see the pieces made by his grandfather. The grandson told me that the cottage was open and apologized that he could not be there in person. We arrived, went in (it was really a great place), photographed the pieces, and left without ever meeting anyone. What trust! Other people also opened their homes to us as the result of a phone call and treated us as family members. For the openness of all those who provided me with information and the opportunity to photograph their homes, I extend a very large thank you.

There are many other people to thank for their assistance with this book. I know that I may have forgotten to include some of you, so please forgive me.

My associate, decorator/stylist Michele Keller, went with me on all the photography shoots. We traveled thousands of miles together. Her sense of style and design was invaluable. She deserves significant credit for the completion of this book.

Others who were very helpful are Bill Pettys, Jerry Sluder, Bob Oestreicher, Charles Copeland, Donald R. Williams, Michael and Anne Toby, Jerry and Jessica Farrell, Jean and Terry Marshal, Connie and Rich Moore, Aly Goodwyn, Barbara Collum, Arden Davis, Emerson Laughner, Linda Davidson, Jack Gunter, the people at FoxFire, Dick Hornburger, Liz and Tim Burdsall, Kathy Pruit, Ralph Lapham, Bob and Melvine Boone, Don Ellis, Elaine Rush, Bob and Gayle Greenhill, Helen Powers, Ted Comstock, Lewis Baer, Bruce Newman, Richard Austin, Maynard Langford, Herb Fink, Rick Cooke, Jane Becker, Steve Zeitels, Ellen Harris, the William Nolan family, the William Knoff family, Herb Chambers, Jenifer Self, Harold Hance, Jonathan Schwartz, Alan Pereske, and Ken Handley.

RALPH KYLLOE, ED. D.

INTRODUCTION

It was 4:30 A.M., and I was stiff and sore from

spending a chilly night in the back of my truck. The air

was misty and cold. Outside, hundreds of moving flash-

lights created an eerie, unreal atmosphere. The flea

market was supposed to open at daybreak, but, as usual, all

the predawn scouting was where the action really began.

Within seconds I had my shoes tied and coat zipped and joined in the hunt. After an exhausting, nonproductive hour of peering under tarps and trying to get a look at small treasures inside still-packed boxes, I stopped to adjust my jacket and noticed a piece of birchbark under a blanket in the back of a truck. I uncovered the piece that turned out to be a shield-shaped mirror covered with birchbark and deer hooves. It was an original Ernest Stowe hall mirror made around 1901. The owner apologized for having to charge me $450 for the piece. I paid his price without negotiation.

The mirror hung in my house for a year, and I later exhibited it, along with many other pieces, at the Museum of Our National Heritage in Lexington, Massachusetts. A few months after the show, I sold the piece for $5,000. Hunting for rustic antiques and the thrill of the "find" is an addictive pastime for thousands, and a stimulating livelihood for a few.

RUSTIC FURNITURE — A BRIEF HISTORY

Significant interest in rustic furnishings and accessories has developed during the past decade. Magazines such as *Country Living, Architectural Digest, Traditional Homes* and many others frequently showcase rustic items. Many museums and private collectors are acquiring rustic articles and, as a result, the prices of such items are escalating dramatically at auctions. At the same time there are presently over twenty-five hundred log-home construction companies around the country, a startling increase over ten years ago. The reason for all this interest is that things rustic have come to be regarded as classical folk art, and people are becoming aware that they have significant relevancy to contemporary society and lifestyles.

Rustic Americana can be defined as items made of twigs, logs, sticks, roots, tree stumps, or branches, and occasionally animal horns and antlers. The bark is left on many of the pieces, and little or no attempt is made to conceal the natural aberrations in the wood. Traditionally rustic pieces, and folk art in general, have been made by untrained artisans and craftspeople, a fact which remains true today. Simple construction techniques and tools were used to create the unique pieces that now are enjoying considerable attention.

In America, rustic furniture first gained popularity during the mid-1800s. At that time the Industrial Revolution, with its low-tech sweatshops, forced people to reevaluate their changing lifestyle. Interest in a simpler, more natural, way of living was popularized through books, articles, and by word of mouth. Consequently, rustic furniture evolved through the efforts of folk artists and craftspeople who catered to the vacation and resort crowd and addressed the issues of life "in a more natural way" by means of their abilities as furniture builders.

Rustic furniture continued to be popular in all parts of the country until the early 1950s, when aluminum and plastic furniture superseded it as the furniture of choice for resorts and residences. A significant revitalization of the rustic style occurred in the 1970s, and today over five hundred people around the country are transforming roots, sticks, twigs, and branches into functional furniture and decorative arts.

Rustic furniture can be found throughout the country, with indigenous materials often dictating the type which is made. The Midwest, specifically Indiana with its vast stands of hickory trees, is a stronghold for hickory furniture and at one time was the home of six different hickory-furniture manufacturers. Builders in the South turn the roots and branches of its multitude of rhododendron and laurel bushes into massive settees, tables, chairs and case pieces (bureaus, cupboards, bookcases, etc.). Craftspeople in Florida create oversized sets of furniture from cypress trees. The northern, wooded region produces items made of birch, cedar, maple and spruce. The Rocky Mountain and Northwest areas have developed huge pieces from lodgepole pines. And the Southwest features articles made from scrub pine and often longhorn steer horns.

Philosophically, rustic furniture seeks to remind both the maker and the user of the ties which connect human beings to the natural world. It brings us back to the woods. It evokes the spirituality of the wild. Rustic furniture and wilderness experiences encourage people to return the artificial world of the Industrial Revolution to a more natural environment and thus these mediums help vitalize the spirit of the urban dweller.

Rustic furniture also embodies an element of defiance and occasionally a touch of arrogance. It is a slap in the face to high technology and social expectations. Rustic furnishings, and often their makers, have always been—by choice—outside of mainstream society.

WHY MAKE RUSTIC FURNITURE?

On the other hand, certain realities are ever present, even for rustic furniture makers. One needs to make a living, and the majority of rustic furniture makers have always been aware of that fact. Guides in the North Woods were kindly told by their employers to "make some furniture" during the cold winter months when the property owners

A B O V E The Eddy Chalet in the White Mountains of New Hampshire was constructed and decorated in the rustic style around the turn of the century. The oversized furniture was constructed of cedar logs cut on the property. Many guests spent happy hours in these mission-influenced Morris chairs situated throughout the hotel.

were not in residence. Many itinerants followed the recreation and vacation routes and made furniture for the many retreats, camps, and lodges that catered to the vacation crowd. Others exchanged room and board for rustic furniture. And still others started making hoop chairs out of hickory poles and wound up having hundreds of employees and manufacturing thousands of pieces of furniture a month for a worldwide clientele.

Interestingly enough, economic conditions have often initiated new efforts in rustic manufacturing. During the Great Depression, many skilled and semiskilled workers were out of work. Since "bare essentials" are all that are needed to construct rustic pieces, and because few peo-

ple had the money for expensive tools and materials, it's not surprising that these people decided to make do with whatever they had to create furniture. As an example, during the depression two major Indiana hickory-furniture companies went out of business, but three others were started. People recognized that it took little talent and less money to start a hickory-furniture business, and with time on their hands, they did just that.

There is another motivation to build rustic furniture, one that exists for all art forms. Many people are simply inspired to create. They try to improve on nature by making something both functional and artistic for its own sake. They are intrinsically motivated to use their own two hands in the process of creation and are driven to become involved with the natural gnarls, twists, and contortions inherent in wood. It is an intriguing fact that many of the accomplished rustic builders today are very talented people who dropped out of corporate society to follow a call to become entrepreneurs and artisans.

THE ART OF RUSTIC

The majority of rustic furniture makers probably did not initially possess the skills and sophistication to create a finished piece of traditional furniture. Probably most of them were also originally unaware of the philosophical implications of their endeavors. But their lack of understanding of the metaphysical or psychological aspects of creating rustic pieces did not prevent them from achieving sophistication in their art form. Rustic is popular today because much of what is produced is classically beautiful, inspirational, and timeless. By this, I mean that many rustic pieces are now considered to be in the realm of higher art and can stand with classical efforts in painting, sculpture, or music.

Not everyone would agree with this opinion, however. In all honesty, many people , upon first seeing Rustic Americana, find it repulsive, strange, grotesque, schizophrenic, and an example of another "realm of weirdness." Sigmund Freud, when

Massive rustic chairs at the Shrine of the Pines in Michigan. The chairs were made from driftwood gathered from the shores of Lake Michigan in the 1920s. The builder of these chairs, with hatchet in hand, stands proudly behind his work.

he first saw rustic furniture, said, "Of all the things I've seen in America, this is the strangest."

Many people who see rustic for the first time find it to be trendy, while others view it in philosophical terms: it inspires them. Some rustic furniture makers, friends of mine, recently exhibited their work in Japan. Modern Japanese people, who had never been exposed to rustic furniture before, were immediately drawn to it. They touched it repeatedly and spent an inordinate amount of time sitting in the chairs and commenting on how beautiful everything was. (The makers of the furniture, needless to say, are quite pleased with

the number of orders they have since received from the Japanese.)

Art, then, is an ethereal phenomenon. It is truly in the eye of the beholder. It is a fleeting impression. It reawakens and stirs senses; it causes pain and joy; it allows us, even forces us, to feel. It transcends our own world and holds us. It brings us together both as individuals and as a society. It is what keeps us going. It is the bond that unites the spiritual and physical realities of the world.

Rustic furniture fuses elements of joy, happiness, and humor. It also often contains elements of anger and other harsher passions. It emanates from another realm, a different place, a more natural, real place where emotions lie on the surface and are not disguised, hidden, or manipulated. Rustic furniture represents a very high form of art that few people appreciate and fewer still understand. Rustic pieces abound with humor, but they also occasionally "make the skin crawl." They can hit instincts that are very primal and call out "the dragons within."

Furniture makers are often very similar in character to the art which they create. One woman, the wife of a rustic furniture maker, described her husband as being "as twisted as the furniture he makes." Many individuals I have met who build rustic furniture are certainly on the edge of society. They are people who may lack social skills and who have tried to, but never quite fit into traditional society. They are very often bright individuals driven by unseen and unheard voices. They are artists and entrepreneurs and generally "get around to things" when they feel like it. They see things others don't. They often have a unique intensity. They are compelled to create.

The real beauty in creating art is that it is available to all of us: a secretary typing a letter, a dishwasher drying dishes, a construction worker, or someone in prison. Victor Frankle, an eminent psychiatrist who survived the Nazi concentration camps, relates a story about a starved inmate who always stayed on his job of building stone fences longer that the other prisoners because he took pride and pleasure in his work. He was an artist and the quality of his life was enhanced through his efforts, even under those most stressful circumstances.

Society is a function of art. Social order has emerged and continues to exist because individuals striving to better themselves come together to enhance the human experience as a whole. Art cannot survive in a vacuum. The personal and social benefits of the artistic endeavor pervade society and are available to all, regardless of what medium they may choose.

RUSTIC ORIGINS

Items of a rustic nature did not originate in America nor within the past century. The first piece of rustic probably emerged when an early humanoid rolled a log over and sat on it in front of a fire.

All cultures have enjoyed rustic artistry. Chinese artwork shows rustic chairs from the tenth century. Rustic artists from England and France have produced wonderful pieces for centuries. Rustic chairs have recently been located in Australia and different provinces in the former USSR. People have also mentioned to me that interesting examples have lately been "discovered" in Africa.

Rustic furniture is usually found in resort and vacation areas. The Adirondack Park, in upstate New York, was the site of unique styles of architecture and furniture produced for the wealthy during the late Victorian and turn-of-the-century periods. Massive settees and rockers made of rhododendron roots can be found on the porches of vacation retreats throughout the Appalachian Mountains. Upstate Michigan, with its lakes and forests, houses many rustic articles similar to those found in the Adirondacks. The Rocky Mountains, although not extensively used as a vacation location during Victorian times, have many old lodges filled with rustic

things. Southwestern rural vacation places have their own brand of rustic furnishings, and items made from huge tree stumps have been found in fishing and hunting camps along the West Coast all the way to Alaska.

Several different categories of Rustic furniture exist: North Woods, Southern root, Indiana hickory, twig, Gypsy, western, antler and taxidermy, and Rocky Mountain rustic. Following is a brief introduction to each type.

NORTH WOODS FURNITURE

North Woods furniture can be found from Maine to Minnesota. This type of furniture is best exemplified by items constructed from tree stumps or branches, with either twig inlay (also referred to as mosaic) or applied birchbark, or a combination of both. Woods used in production include white and yellow birch, red cedar, alder and cherry twigs, and other materials indigenous to the area.

It is often thought that the Adirondacks is the place where North Woods rustic furniture originated. No doubt the Adirondack artisans made a significant and lasting contribution. Nonetheless, identical styles and examples from the same time period have been located throughout the North Woods region.

North Woods furnishings were inspired by similar, earlier efforts in Europe. Classical examples of twig inlay or mosaic work have appeared in England, France, Yugoslavia, and other areas. These European pieces significantly predate North Woods rustic. It is also interesting to note that pieces from Europe appear to have more sophisticated construction techniques then their American counterparts. For instance, all of the European case pieces that I have had the opportunity to examine were joined with dovetailing rather than nails.

Rustic furnishings from the North Woods area include everything from intricate birchbark and mosaic picture frames to massive dining-room sets, beds, lighting, and everything else needed to complete an entire house. Huge log homes were constructed and a significant North Woods lifestyle evolved. The best known of the estates include Camp Uncas, Pine Knot, Sagamore, Kamp Kill Kare and other great camps in the Adirondacks, as well as Granot Loma in upstate Michigan, probably the most lavish of all. The well-known furniture makers from the early part of this century from this region include Ernest Stowe, Lee Fountain, George Wilson, Clarence Nichols, and many others.

Twig mosaic work represents the ultimate artistry of the North Woods effort. The intricate inlay and designs produced on the tables, case pieces, and other items reflect traditional folk-art motifs such as the star, schoolhouse, and basket designs, as well as numerous geometric patterns. The actual shapes of the case pieces and other furnishings are quite innovative and were often dictated by the natural qualities of the materials used in construction. Nonetheless, the occasional influence of Gothic, Eastlake, Victorian and other styles is evident.

Two commercial ventures associated with North Woods furniture are receiving attention today. The Rittenhouse Company was started by John Rittenhouse in 1929. His family had been active in the telephone-pole railroad business during the 1800s, and custom-made rustic furniture seemed a logical choice for son John. His furniture was basically made out of peeled pine poles and finished using either shellac or varnish. The furniture's unique feature was its construction out of half-round logs instead of the usual flat-cut boards. Although his company usually had fewer than ten employees, John Rittenhouse still offered a full line of camp furniture, including pieces for the bedroom, dining room, and living room. The pieces are signed with a paper label that reads "Genuine Rittenhouse Furniture." The Rittenhouse Company was located in Cheboygan, Michigan, where it is today considered quite desirable. The furniture was never intended to be expensive, but rather good, clean camp items that could be affordable to those wanting useful items for a second home.

The New Jersey Fence Company, located in Burlington, New Jersey, offered a very extensive line of outdoor rustic items made of white cedar. Their products, which they called Lincraft Rustic, included not only birdhouses, but fences, gazebos, pergolas, furniture, and complete log cabins. They sold these things through various East Coast distributors and mail-order catalogs. The one catalog that is still available is dated 1929. Their products appear to be very well designed and constructed, and every so often, I have purchased one of their pieces from one of the many East Coast resorts.

SOUTHERN ROOT FURNISHINGS

Southern root and other rustic items were created from the early 1820s to the mid-1930s in or near the Appalachian Mountains. The pieces were generally constructed from either rhododendron or laurel bushes or their roots. A common practice was for someone to make a few items at home, then load them onto a wagon and sell the pieces door-to-door at the various resort centers throughout the southern mountain ranges. This method of marketing was a favorite amongst the many Gypsy families residing in the South. Other times craftspeople would construct items on-site and exchange their labor and creativity for room and board.

Many different styles evolved throughout the southern region. The Gypsies developed their own unique line of chairs with dramatic circular backs and straight arms. Other artisans were influenced by established styles. One gentleman from North Carolina mentioned that his grandfather, who was a prolific rustic furniture maker, often sought inspiration in the pages of the ever-present Sears and Roebuck catalog and copied whatever "suited his fancy." Rustic patterns were also influenced by Gothic, Victorian, and period designs, as well as the styles of Michael Thonet of Austria and others. Along with expanding on old styles and creating new forms of furniture, southern makers frequently embellished their products with regional touches such as chip carving (also known as rustication), unique painting designs, and other types of decorations.

INDIANA HICKORY FURNITURE

Indiana was the site of six different rustic furniture companies. The largest and oldest of these firms was the Old Hickory Chair Company, which was started in Martinsville, Indiana, in 1892. This firm was founded by Billy Richardson, a barnyard craftsman whose descendants still reside in nearby Morgantown, Indiana. Other companies that produced hickory-bark furniture were the Jasper Hickory Furniture Company of Jasper, Indiana; the Rustic Hickory Furniture Company of Laporte, Indiana (started and owned by E. F. Handley, whose grandchildren still reside in Laporte); and the Columbus Hickory Furniture Company (owned by L. A. Simmons, who also started the Wig Wam motel chain), which later moved to Bedford, Indiana. Martinsville was also the location of a second hickory company, The Indiana Willow Products Company, which was started by former employees of Old Hickory, Emerson Laughner and Clyde Hatley. The state prison in Putnamville did a thriving business in hickory furniture as well. There were at least three other very small start-up companies, but they failed to make inroads into the market.

The major companies did extensive business and shipped items all over the world. At its peak, the Old Hickory Company of Martinsville was producing two thousand pieces per week and shipped boxcars to the Adirondacks on a weekly basis. Old Hickory finally went out of business in 1965, when it became apparent that it was becoming too costly to compete with aluminum and plastic porch furniture.

Today the Old Hickory Furniture Company has been revitalized and is back in business, making both contemporary and classically designed rustic furniture. Two other firms are also making hickory furniture, one in Flatrock, Indiana, and the other in Georgia. The State of Indiana is also once again manufacturing hickory furniture at the prison in Putnamville.

TWIG FURNITURE

Bent-twig chairs are known to have been made all along the East Coast and in the Midwest. The most famous and recognizable of the designs are chairs and rockers made by the Amish in Pennsylvania, Ohio, and Indiana. Bent-twig chairs appear to have originated around the turn of the century. These chairs are generally constructed from willow branches and have oak and occasionally maple slat seats.

Because of their dramatic contours, these chairs are frequently described as the most comfortable ever made. First-time observers are always amazed by the way the chairs seem to fit their bodies, despite their uncomfortable appearance. It has been noted that there is a strong similarity between bentwood rockers and the chairs made by the Austrian designer Michael Thonet, who is famous for his innovations in the bentwood style. No doubt the Amish, many of whom immigrated from Germany and Austria, were influenced by these early Austrian efforts.

Amish families in northern Indiana and other parts of the country still manufacture bentwood rockers in the same styles and using the same techniques as they did generations ago. It is fascinating to watch Amish craftspeople work with natural materials and techniques that have been passed down for many years. You feel as if you have taken a step back in history.

The Amish were certainly not the only makers of twig rockers. Many fine examples exist in designs completely different from the Amish ones. Many twig rockers, for instance, have huge swirls incorporated into them. Others are highly decorated with chip carving that adds dramatically to their appearance, and still others are of different designs that depict the area in which they were made. Some are painted with colors and motifs which also reflect different regions.

GYPSY CHAIRS

As mentioned earlier, the Gypsies developed their own style of rustic chairs. These chairs had large, sweeping circular backs and were usually constructed from wil-low trees indigenous to the southern Appalachian area. The usual marketing strategy employed by Gypsy families was for them to show up at someone's home and offer to make furniture in exchange for meals that day. They were quite successful at introducing their styles, which were soon copied by other rustic furniture makers. It is thought that the type of chair most often associated with the Gypsies was originally inspired by a design brought over from Africa.

Many people around the country are still making this style of chair today. The classical lines of these chairs have long made them a favorite for front porches and shady spots conducive to moments of quiet and solitude.

WESTERN RUSTIC FURNITURE

A true western style of rustic furniture was late in developing. However, we have to think of massive chairs and settees made from the horns of longhorn steers as truly western. Horn furniture came to prominence in Texas in the 1880s. Wenzel Friedrich began making horn chairs, settees, and tables during that period, and his designs were so original that he won numerous national awards. A few companies in Chicago also thrived by making horn chairs. This is not surprising, considering that the stockyards in that city were the largest in the world and horns were plentiful.

Occasionally in the Southwest, one finds items constructed from scrub pine trees, but in general, with the exception of horn furniture, rustic furniture making in Texas and the Southwest was not extensive.

ANTLER AND TAXIDERMY ITEMS

Pieces constructed from, or adorned with, antlers, horns, hoofs and other taxidermy can also be included in the rustic genre. Such items were frequently made in Switzerland, Scotland, Austria, and the Black Forest region. Items from these areas included chandeliers, gun racks, pen-and-ink desk sets, chairs, and a variety of other decorative things.

Americans also made items that included taxidermy. Lamps, mirrors, and coatracks were adorned with deer hooves. Beds, bureaus, desks, and office chairs also incorporated antlers and other taxidermy parts. Taxidermy was also a part of the decoration of almost all rustic homes, lodges, and camps as souvenirs of the hunt.

Today several companies manufacture products featuring naturally shed antler, and it is quite common to see antler chandeliers, tables, desks, chairs, and similar pieces pictured in magazines which display contemporary interiors.

ROCKY MOUNTAIN RUSTIC FURNITURE

Until the 1930s, most retreats in the Rocky Mountains were decorated with either mission or Victorian furnishings. At that time, Thomas Canada Molesworth, a "homemade"-furniture maker, was commissioned to decorate a huge rustic retreat. For this job Molesworth created furniture from burled pine poles. His chairs, settees, and other pieces were adorned with Indian and western motifs. His oversized and innovative rustic designs were soon copied by others, and many ranches, hotels, and lodges were soon filled with Molesworth-inspired furniture.

Rocky Mountain rustic, or cowboy furniture, as it is occasionally called today, has seen a dramatic revival recently, and several companies are turning out massive beds, case pieces, chandeliers, tables, chairs, and other pieces to furnish the many new log homes, resorts, restaurants, and other retreats that are being built in the mountain and western states.

RUSTIC DECORATIVE ITEMS

Rustic decorative items of every conceivable nature have been mass-produced as tourist souvenirs, in school woodworking classes, and as scouting projects, among other reasons. Indians in Maine, Michigan,

ABOVE Rustic furniture was frequently used in advertising efforts during the Victorian period. Here, the Dodge Skating Company of Rhode Island uses a root settee to add interest to their new Silver King ice skates.

Canada, and other locales made items to sell to tourists, including birchbark canoes and picture frames, wastebaskets, and other curios. Boy Scouts made miniature log cabins and birdhouses. Inmates in prisons made all sorts of rustic collectibles, including furniture and birchbark items. Craftspeople from all over made miniature canoe paddles, clocks, bookends, twig stands, lighting, and many other interesting rustic decorations. Today such items are considered collectible.

One surprising discovery is that there was no significant rustic output in the timber regions of the

Northwest. Efforts to locate historic rustic furniture builders in this area have proven fruitless, and only a few Indiana hickory pieces and stump-based items have been located. Nonetheless, there are a number of builders today making stunning lodgepole furniture in California, Washington, and Oregon.

Because of the resurgence in the desire to live more closely with nature, and because rustic is now being regarded as a major folk-art form, many people around the world are integrating the rustic into their lifestyles. This more natural way of life may include plants and animals in the home, rustic furniture on the porch, or stunning log homes that blend with the environment. Decorators are realizing that not only does rustic furniture blend well with many other styles, but it is also comfortable and functional. Many restaurants and clothing stores are incorporating rustic accessories into their decor and inventory as it gains popularity.

Nationwide, people are recognizing that the rustic style has significant appeal to individuals who seek a life closer to nature.

ROOMS FOR LIVING

LEFT   This contemporary living room in Maine effectively utilizes new and antique furniture to make a striking statement. The mantle holds a collection of Indian baskets, canoes, and "fungus art." The antique twig mosaic mirror came from New York. The Indiana Hickory armchair is period 1920s, and the contemporary armchair is by Barry Gregson of the Adirondacks. The 1920s table lamp with mica inserts is from the Old Hickory Company; the drop-leaf table is by Gustav Stickley.

ustic living rooms have the

capacity to renew the spirit. They are intended to

provide comfort and to foster a sense of community and

family among those who share them. A living room

is where you can let down your guard and relax.

Traditional "work" is not allowed in this room.

Bold, dramatic chairs made in the Adirondacks, the Northwest, the West, and other parts of the country offer people the chance to relax in comfort.

Reading, conversation, listening to music, and enjoyment of other art forms is encouraged. People only a few blinks away from sleep can find peace and solitude. Under certain circumstances, living rooms are ideal for casual, intimate conversations with friends and family. These are places where individuals become groups and where groups find acceptance.

Comfort and livability are the keys to a great living room. Sofas are not covered in plastic. Feet and beverages are not out of place on the coffee table. The family pets are invited to cuddle with their owners on any one of the chairs or couches. Lamp shades of mica, glass, cloth, or parchment sport a host of rustic scenes. Canoes hang from the ceiling, and the fireplace is usually roaring.

It is surprising to discover how many rustic or vacation homes that were built in the early part of the century have been decorated with Arts and Crafts (e.g., mission) furniture. Most mission furniture is virtually indestructible and is consistent in philosophy with the rustic movement. Large mission settees look great with their leather upholstery and Indian-blanket throw pillows. Today much of this furniture has been reupholstered in a variety of coverings, including Native American and Pendleton patterns and other rustic colors and styles.

It is also important to remember that many vacation homes were really second homes, and that even the most spectacular of them became repositories for hand-me-down or unwanted furniture. It is ironic that the owners of almost all turn-of-the-century vacation homes were quite wealthy and often transferred their unwanted furnishings to their retreats. Fortunately for us, most of these people had good taste as well as financial resources. As a result, the majority of these early rustic retreats were very eclectic in style and frequently were adorned with Tiffany lamps and designer wicker, rustic, mission, Victorian and other high-end items.

SOFAS AND CHAIRS

Comfortable rustic couches, apart from those made of Indiana hickory or in mission style, are very difficult to find. Consequently, many homes today have new upholstered sofas that are often the focal point of the room. The most comfortable always seem to be those that are oversized and give one the sensation of sinking into a cloud or pillow. Many rustic homes have sleeper sofas for guests who happen to show up on weekends for an extended visit.

Single chairs are also a necessity. Many of the older turn-of-the-

LEFT The settee is part of a thirty-piece root set, ca. 1930s, presently in the lobby of the Lake Rabun Hotel, Lakemont, Georgia. The settee made of cedar poles and coffee table of rhododendron branches are frequently used by guests, who find the pillowy green leather cushions relaxingly comfortable.

century homes used not only mission seating such as Morris chairs, armchairs and rockers, but also very elegant wicker pieces of either Bar Harbor or Victorian design. Indiana hickory chairs were also used extensively in rustic or vacation settings. The Old Hickory Company, one of two Martinsville, Indiana, firms, shipped boxcars of furniture from their plant every day, and their peak production was about two thousand pieces per week. When we consider that this company was in business for over seventy years, it is easy to see why so much hickory furniture is still in use. And Old Hickory was only one of six different companies manufacturing this type of furniture.

Because Indiana hickory pieces, when cared for properly, are almost indestructible and because they exemplify excellent design, it is quite practical for many people to make use of these pieces today. Hickory lounge chairs, armchairs, rockers, beds, and numerous other pieces fit into the rustic setting quite well and blend very naturally with the mission and wicker furniture which often accompanies them.

At the same time, however difficult to find, other types of comfortable and aesthetically pleasing rustic chairs, both antique and new, are making their way into many homes. Bold, dramatic chairs made in the Adirondacks, the Northwest, the West, and other parts of the country offer people the chance to relax in comfort.

TABLES

Small occasional tables are essential to any living room. Rustic tables in many forms, woods, and styles are presently on the market. These tables are ideal for displaying the varied collections that passionate people seem to revel in assembling. Collections of miniature canoes, doll-size rustic furniture, birchbark accessories, canoe paddles, and numerous other items are naturally and proudly displayed on tables made of birch, cedar, hickory, driftwood and other woods.

Tables in the rustic genre take many forms. Stump- or root-based tables are made by digging up small-to-medium trees, cutting the roots so that they are stable and level, and adding a top of either trimmed mosaic or plain boards. Other tables are created by simply cutting appropriate branches, attaching a top, and finishing the piece with various decorative touches.

Although almost all styles of rustic furniture are dictated by the materials selected by the builder, it is not uncommon for tables and other pieces to be influenced by other styles of furniture developed throughout history. A man once mentioned to me that his grandfather, a prolific rustic furniture maker, was a master of his craft. Unfortunately, this builder was not as creative with his designs as with his hammer. When he was about to construct a new piece, he would simply open an old Sears and Roebuck catalog and copy one of the styles pictured on the furniture pages.

FIREPLACES

Fireplaces and fires are an integral part of the rustic atmosphere. No outdoor or camp scene is complete without one. Fires are so important as a means of bonding and relaxing that in the past, if a house did not have a fireplace, artificial logs and red light bulbs were combined to fabricate a fire in an artificial fireplace complete with a mantel.

Real fireplaces need andirons and fire screens. In the past, rustic andirons took the shape of owls, pine trees, Indian tepees, and other creative designs. Many fire screens were also adorned with rustic scenes, including log homes and fishing and forest panoramas which were applied to the wire mesh that

ABOVE This contemporary home is decorated with high-end European antiques, including paintings. The simple birch chair from the Adirondacks blends well with the many plants placed throughout the house.

ABOVE The table is about a hundred years old and is made of roots applied along a tree stump. Toy root chairs were probably made by Joseph Quinn of Virginia. The elk-hoof lamp with mica shade is ca. 1930s.

protects the room from embers. Both rustic andirons and fire screens are being reproduced today, or originals can be found in flea markets, at auctions, or in antique shops.

Fireplace mantels are as important to rustic decor as fireplaces. Trophies, either won, caught or bought, look totally at home gracing the shelves above a fireplace. Photos of all sorts, personal memorabilia, snowshoes, skis, canoe paddles, and other artifacts fit in perfectly with the rustic feel of a fireplace.

LIGHTING

Lighting is also very important to the rustic setting. Colors emitted from lamps should be soft, subtle and unobtrusive. The brightest light that should ever be allowed in a rustic home is bursts of color from sunrises and sunsets.

Rustic floor and table lamps are made from burls, sturdy branches, roots, bark and other parts of trees. A variety of lamps are also made from the naturally shed antlers of elk, deer, moose and other animals. Many taxidermy facilities in the past made lamps from the hooves of animals and then adorned them with shades depicting various rustic scenes.

Also popular is antique lighting in the mission and prairie-school styles. Table and floor lamps, sconces, and chandeliers made by

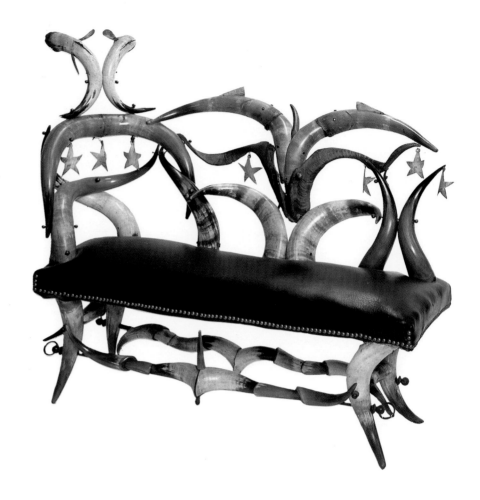

RIGHT This horn lounge chair was probably constructed by Wenzel Friedrich during the Victorian period. Friedrich resided in Texas and won many national awards for his innovative forms and designs. Horn furniture today is considered very dramatic and is difficult to find.

Gustav Stickley, Dirk Van Erp, Charles Limbert and others are stunning additions to any rustic room. Lighting by Greene and Greene, Frank Lloyd Wright, and other prairie-school designers contributes a sense of power and intrigue to homes. Many people are also using antique lighting by Tiffany, Handel, Pairpoint, and other turn-of-the-century glass and lamp manufacturers. The colors filtered through these lamps are truly stunning and compliment any room. If you can't find or afford antique lamps, all of these styles are being reproduced today with effects quite similar to their older cousins.

Some people have successfully adapted old lanterns, Rayo and other kerosene lamps, as well as Gone-with-the-Wind lamps and student lamps to light their homes. Green cased-glass shades, often used by the Emerlite Company, provide excellent diffusion for lamps or chandeliers. The warm green glow cast by these lamp shades adds a touch of nature to the rustic ambience of the room.

ACCESSORIES

Accessory pieces of furniture can enhance the living room. Rustic magazine holders, coat trees, shelving, log holders, tea carts, tall cased clocks, ottomans, corner cupboards, and many other items add to the charm of the room and help create a lived-in atmosphere.

Art enriches our lives. If we decorate our living room and the rest of the rooms in our home with the intention of turning them into works of art, then those who experience the place where we live will share the effects of our artistic endeavors.

ABOVE   A reverse-painted Handel lamp adds drama to the contemporary home where it resides. The lamp rests on a Victorian root table and is surrounded by antique Old Hickory furniture. Reverse-painted lamps often have wonderful rustic scenes on them and are easy to find.

REVEREND BEN MARCUS DAVIS

Ben Davis was born in Burnsville, North Carolina, in 1887. By profession he was an ordained Southern Baptist circuit minister. He traveled by carriage and horseback to the many different revival meetings held in the far western areas of North Carolina. Once he rode in a car but was unfortunately hit by a Coca-Cola truck, so he never again rode in a motorized vehicle. ❦ According to his grandson, Davis was a quiet, gentle man. He was very industrious, had the mind of an engineer, and was a great role model for his eight children. His sermons were not of the fire-and-brimstone type, but rather were calm orations on the virtues of good living. He frequently stayed for weeks with different families when out on the preaching circuit. In exchange for room and board, he often gave presents of things he made. He was very well-liked and was highly respected. ❦ As Thomas Molesworth is in the West and Ernest Stowe is in the North, Davis is recognized as the premier rustic builder of the South. He spent hours each day collecting small laurel roots and branches in the mountains of North Carolina. He dried them carefully in the sun and split them in half before adorning the many chairs, tables, sideboards, cabinets, beds, rocking chairs, book shelves, and other pieces he made. Prior to their application, he would chip-carve each piece with a small pen knife. He would often spend a full year on one dining-room set that he would give away as a wedding present. He once decorated a huge pulpit in a church which, unfortunately, burned to the ground. ❦ Davis's furniture is stunning. Each piece was of his own design and was meticulously crafted. The frames were made of rough-cut chestnut that he spent hours sanding. The hardware was always the same, purchased at a nearby five-and-dime store. The furniture tends to be small in scale, perhaps because Davis was only five feet eight inches tall and made the pieces to his liking. In later years, Davis constructed tabletops of plywood, and today these pieces have aged to a rich golden brown. ❦ In the late 1930s, Davis stopped building furniture, but he continued preaching for many more years. His grandson remembers his swollen, arthritic hands and his calm ways. He died of a nose bleed at age eighty-one.

RIGHT Sideboard by Reverend Ben Davis is used in a room accented with creels, a moose-antler clock, and toy hickory furniture.

ABOVE This drop-front desk dates to the turn of the century and was found in Maine. The interior of the desk has numerous cubby holes and drawers. The patterns in the mosaic twigwork blend well with the geometric schemes of Native American designs.

LEFT Probably the most intricate rustic armchair ever built, this piece was found in Michigan and dates from about 1910. The original 1930s advertising piece is from the Old Hickory company. A rich red Hudson Bay blanket adds necessary color to the room.

ABOVE Rhododendron-root table serves as a
resting point for a variety of collections and a
Victorian lamp.

ABOVE The pair of Gothic rockers came originally from Maine and today offer rest and ambience in a significant house in New Jersey. The planter is of European origin.

RIGHT This table has about fifteen hundred tiny roots applied to the base. The table was made at the turn of the century in the Finger Lakes region of central New York. The stark simplicity and intensity of the piece make it the focal point of the room.

ABOVE A Gustav Stickley sideboard is the resting place for an original Limbert table lamp. A very rare pair of antler boxes surround the lamp and offer a place to store personal items. The contemporary armchair is by Barry Gregson. Native American artifacts bring a sense of wilderness and adventure to this home.

RIGHT Contemporary chairs occupy an intimate corner that is warmed by a fireplace. The Native American rugs and blankets contribute bold colors and patterns to the setting. Birch frames and collectibles rest on the mantel.

ABOVE   The chip-carved settee was constructed by Reverend Ben Davis of the Asheville, North Carolina, area in the 1920s. It has been reupholstered with Indian blankets. The Indiana Hickory lamp and mica shade are from the 1920s.

LEFT   The captain's chair and drop-leaf, gate-leg table, which are quite rare, were made by the Old Hickory Furniture Company during the 1930s. The lamp is constructed of a single hickory pole and has a turn-of-the-century mica shade. The antique fishing creels, Adirondack basket, packs, leather ski boots, and a fishing net add a finishing touch to the surroundings.

ABOVE Part of the thirty-piece set at the Lake Rabun Hotel in Georgia. Guests often rest in the comfortable armchair and settee. Dark green throw pillows blend well with the natural colors of the furniture.

RIGHT The warm colors of the aged wood in this console table and mirror from the Lake Rabun Hotel blend dramatically into the surroundings.

ABOVE A Bavarian antler console table blends nicely with aged, warm pine boards. The table serves as a display piece for arrangements of Majolica, sea-shell art, and other collectibles. The table is Victorian.

LEFT Two dramatic high-end rustic chairs offer study space in this room. The antique birch chair is from the Adirondacks, the mosaic table is from Maine, the Gothic chair is probably Southern, and the chandelier is from Germany.

ABOVE Living room in a small Indiana house holds an unusual collection of accessories. The reclining chair and ottoman were made by prison inmates in the 1930s. Syrian table lamp is ca. 1910. The pastel colors of the Rainbow pottery blend nicely with the rustic surroundings. Indian kachina dolls rest atop a corner cupboard.

RIGHT A pair of original Lee Fountain rockers receive constant use in this Adirondack retreat that overlooks Lake George. Birch trim was applied throughout the house.

A B O V E Toys and other collectibles are
displayed on a rhododendron table.

R I G H T Indian blankets and oriental throw
pillows add comfort and color to the room,
which contains an Arts and Crafts-style sofa
made by the Old Hickory Company around the
1930s. The birch Victrola is originally from
Michigan. (Photo © 1993 by George Bouret)

STUDIES & DENS

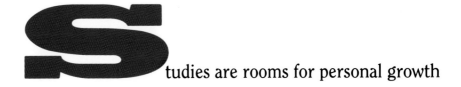tudies are rooms for personal growth

and enlightenment. They are also rooms where neces-

sary work is completed. These are the rooms for books

and business deals, quiet times and phone calls, creative

ideas and solitude. Rustic decor in this room fosters

dreams that allow natural creativity to emerge.

OPPOSITE The geometric patterns in the base of this 1920s desk suggest a prairie-school influence. The desk was found recently at a flea market in Ohio. The turn-of-the-century elk- and moose-antler floor lamp has a mica shade. The desk lamp, constructed of bronze and with a sterling silver inlay indicative of the Art Nouveau period, is from the Heinz Art Metal Shop of Buffalo, New York, ca. 1910.

Studies are rooms for creativity, effort and personal enjoyment. Decorated in the rustic style, they become havens and dens for natural curiosity, exploration and accomplishment.

DESKS

Sturdy, functional desks come in a range of rustic woods. Commercially produced desks of Indiana hickory have long met the needs of individuals seeking a space to work. Adirondack and other rustic builders have created massive desks out of huge logs and rough-cut boards. Other more intricate desks have been built with numerous cubbyholes, drawers, and drop-front writing surfaces. These large, decorative desks not only provide work and organization space but are often the focal point of the room.

SHELVES

Bookcases and other types of rustic shelving are built to last. These items are designed in both simple and complex forms. And it is not uncommon in many homes to see built-in bookcases and shelves that are ideal for displaying large libraries, trophies and personal memorabilia. In general, shelving is constructed of cedar, birch, hickory or twigs in many shapes that facilitate the organizing of papers and documents.

LIGHTING

Functional lighting in the study is a necessity. Many of the lamp fixtures already mentioned fit nicely in the study or office. Nonetheless, many individuals have found other turn-of-the-century lighting fixtures to be both pleasant and workable. Extension, gooseneck, swing arm, and other industrial lamps by the O. C. White Company, as well as desk lamps by Emeralite, Verdelite and others, look quite wonderful with their dark green shades illuminating the workspace.

CHAIRS AND COUCHES

Desk chairs come in many styles and have been constructed of roots, branches, and antlers from steer, elk and deer. Although at first glance chairs made from antlers and horns look uncomfortable, it is pleasantly surprising to discover how functional and intriguing they really are.

Comfortable reading chairs are also important to a study. It is not uncommon to find mission-style Morris chairs and other turn-of-the-century upholstered seating in the den. New or antique oversized wing chairs with ottomans are also quite commonly mixed with rustic furnishings in the personal setting of a den.

Many people also include sofas, settees or couches in their studies. Adorned with pillows, these pieces of furniture are ideal for a late-afternoon nap or an evening with the classics.

ACCESSORIES

Many studies have ceilings high enough to suspend not only large chandeliers but other interesting decorative accessories as well. Nothing is more dramatic than an early birchbark or ribbed canoe hanging from the rafters. Other hangable items range from dogsleds and totem poles to rowboats and sculling oars. Suspended artifacts can add intrigue to the setting of a study or any other area of the home.

Only the imagination limits the height of creativity. One innovative couple painted the ceiling of their den sky blue and filled it with white billowing clouds. The effect was stunning, as the room was designed to display the sunrise and sunset through the windows each morning and evening.

Studies are rooms for creativity, effort and personal enjoyment. Decorated in the rustic style, they become havens and dens for natural curiosity, exploration and accomplishment.

LEFT The desk has the appearance of a prairie-school design and was made about 1910 by the Rustic Hickory Furniture Company of Laporte. The desk chair, newly reupholstered, is mid-Victorian and came from the Black Forest region of Europe. The antique floor lamp is by Old Hickory and has an antique mica shade. A Tiffany art-glass shade tops the desk lamp, manufactured by the O. C. White Company.

ABOVE Lee Fountain made this table and chairs around 1910. Fountain was probably the most prolific rustic builder in the Adirondacks, and his style influences many rustic builders today. Contained in this study is a wonderful fifty-year collection of literature relating to Adirondack tales, fables and history.

ABOVE   The monastic starkness of this room contrasts many other rustic rooms filled to abundance with accessories. The birch stump-based table and cedar wall clock are from the Adirondacks. The root shelving is a classic example of southern root work. Memory vases fill the shelves.

A B O V E Cowboy and Indian artifacts add
character and style to this study in New Jersey.
The chair is Southern and the desk is Adirondack.
A bold Indian rug provides a splash of color.

A B O V E This bold root chair was originally found in New Hampshire and came with a matching settee. The settee went to a museum exhibit and found a home in Colorado. The chair is presently on Nantucket Island. The 1930s floor lamp is by the Bedford Hickory Furniture Company.

L E F T Mosaic desk found originally at a flea market in Massachusetts. There are several cubbyholes in the gallery as well as sectional drawers in the banks of the piece. The desk is lit with a Handel table lamp and the user sits in an Old Hickory chair.

LEFT   This contemporary root chair and table were made by Jerry Farrell of New York State. The picture frame was also made by Farrell, and the bear painting is by Jessica Farrell. The pieces are presently displayed in the Farrells' Victorian home.

RIGHT   Certainly the most dramatic rustic reclining lounge chair around today, this piece is painted on the front and back with rustic scenes and signed "The Criminal." Constructed during the turn of the century, the piece makes a bold statement.

ABOVE   The small desk serves as a phone station off the kitchen in a large log cabin. The desk is from Maine and the hand-made chair was found in Indiana.

ABOVE This study utilizes a turn-of-the-century oak desk and file cabinet as the primary pieces. The massive desk chair is made of elk antlers and was originally found in Michigan. The leather seat has been replaced. The table lamp is birch with a mica shade. The log cabin doll-house church was found in Michigan and has more than twenty movable pieces inside. The waste basket was made by the Old Hickory Company around 1930.

A B O V E This den is often the focal point for quiet times in a large summer home. The antique birch desk is from the Adirondacks and the twig rocker is Southern. Rustic accents compliment the room.

R I G H T Fullness and form make this horn armchair dramatic. The chair and a matching ottoman were found originally in Canada. The seat has been recovered.

LEFT This rustic den is furnished with chairs from the Old Hickory Company, as well as unusual items such as the burled lamp. Kilim Turkish rugs are quickly becoming popular for their vibrant colors and modest price tags.

ABOVE Original foreman's desk used in the Old Hickory factory between 1905 and 1920. It was recently found in a basement of a grandson of one of the former Old Hickory employees. The use of antique taxidermy, trophies, snowshoes, textiles and photos add intensity to the setting. An original Ernest Stowe birch frame hangs in the hall.

LEFT Studies need bookcases. This contemporary piece by Lionel Maurier is constructed in the style of Ernest Stowe.

RIGHT Owners of this study in Indiana utilized a number of Native American artifacts, along with hickory furniture, to create a warm, comfortable room.

ABOVE   One of the most dramatic antler chairs ever made was discovered in Michigan and is surprisingly comfortable. The corner cupboard was produced by the Old Hickory Furniture Company in 1934. Rustic accessories surround the pieces and add ambience to the setting.

LEFT Lee Fountain made this table/book-shelf around 1920 at his workshop in the Adirondacks. This is the only known example of this table design, although Fountain was known to experiment with different prototypes. A turn-of-the-century lamp lights the area.

RIGHT The root sideboard is part of an eleven-piece set, probably made near Asheville, North Carolina, around the 1920s.

A B O V E   Desk and armchair by Ernest Stowe of the Adirondacks. The interior of the desk has
numerous drawers and cubbyholes. The desk was completed in 1904.

R I G H T   This dramatic antique desk is part of a twelve-piece set which also includes some porch
furniture. The craftsman who built the furniture also constructed the entire house in the 1920s.

A B O V E An extremely rare desk set made in 1910 by the Old Hickory Chair Company for an Adirondack Great Camp. The furniture has mellowed to a rich golden brown and is still used by the family who originally purchased the set.

A B O V E A pair of rhododendron armchairs and magazine holder from the North Carolina region. The furniture is surprisingly comfortable and reminds one of the house where the three bears lived.

ABOVE Armchair by Clifford Monteith of Michigan and antique lamp by Old Hickory. The natural wood tones of the furniture blend quite well with the finish on the walls.

RUSTIC EATING AREAS

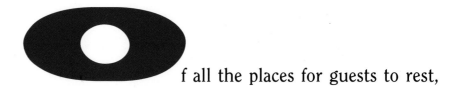

O f all the places for guests to rest,

they seem to like my kitchen the best," goes the old

proverb. Rooms where eating takes place are the focal

points of the home. The television is turned off, the

guests are seated, and the great ritual of the shared meal

is about to begin. Rustic dining rooms are places of

OPPOSITE   Indiana hickory blends naturally with the high vaulted ceilings and a mission chandelier.

Rustic cupboards were made in the early days in the Appalachians, the Adirondacks and many other areas around the country.

comfort and communication, places to tell the stories of today and discuss the dreams of tomorrow. They are rooms that encourage families and friends to come together.

DINING TABLES

The rustic dining table is extremely versatile: here tasty meals are served, the paper is read, homework is completed, and the fishing tackle for tomorrow's outing can be cleaned and prepared. Rustic tables can be massive, large enough to serve a banquet to the neighborhood, or small and dainty, perfect for a candlelight dinner for two. The larger tables have legs made from huge apple-tree branches, rhododendron roots, or cedar or birch trees. Small tables are often scaled-down versions of their heftier cousins and are occasionally adorned with twig supports to add grace and sturdiness, as well as an aesthetic touch.

Comfortable antique tables made by the six different Indiana hickory companies are usually available at antique shops in rustic vacation areas. Don't feel compelled to refinish your table because it has stains or scratches or someone's initials carved in it. Old and rugged is charming and adds to the lived-in effect. If you'd rather have a new table, a range of sizes and shapes are available from rustic builders

around the country. Old or new, don't forget to wax, oil or varnish your table once a year to keep it waterproof.

DINING CHAIRS

The most common sets of dining-room chairs available are usually ones made of hickory in Indiana. Whether old or new, these chairs have been mass produced by the thousands and are quite functional. There are also many very talented individuals around the country making new rustic chairs in a variety of woods and designs.

The most important considerations when choosing dining chairs are comfort and durability. Sit in all the chairs. Do they feel tight? Are they comfortable? Do any of the spindles stick you in the back? Will they last? Is the wood damaged? Remember that wood used in rustic furnishings is not highly processed or finished, so when considering either buying or building them, comfort and condition are the first priorities.

SIDEBOARDS & CUPBOARDS

Almost all dining areas have some sort of sideboard, server or buffet for storage. Most frequently used, because of their availability, are mission pieces made by Stickley, Limbert, Roycroft or other lesser-known Arts and Crafts designers. There are also all sorts of country-pine cupboards, pie safes and cupboards made by Hoosiers in Indiana that work well in the rustic dining area.

In addition, antique rustic servers and cupboards are highly valued today. Rustic cupboards were made in the early days in the Appalachians, the Adirondacks and many other areas around the country. Builders in the southern states made cabinets and adorned them with tiny chip-carved rhododendron roots and other branches. North Woods rustic furniture makers from Maine to Minnesota constructed massive serving and storage pieces out of birch and cedar logs. Craftsmen from the Far West made a variety of cabinets out of pine poles, and the builders in Indiana used hickory poles in the many shapes of their cabinets. Antique European cupboards made of walnut and frequently adorned with antlers are also often used today.

Old rustic cupboards are difficult to find and quite expensive when they are available, however. If you happen to see an antique sideboard that strikes your fancy, you may want to contact one of the new rustic furniture builders and have a copy made. It will save you significant time and money.

Today rustic cupboards are

ABOVE Charming, diminutive corner cupboard by Reverend Ben Davis. The piece is presently owned by his granddaughter in North Carolina.

ABOVE Dining set has five chairs, a table, sideboard, hat tree, magazine holder, and lamp stand. The set was probably made in the Asheville, North Carolina, area around 1920.

being constructed from all types of materials, and you can come up with a realm of innovative ideas by discussing your project with your local craftsperson. Better yet, find an old cupboard and have a craftsperson trim the piece with twigs and birchbark. Many people are choosing to do this now, and the furniture looks great.

LIGHTING

Lighting is an essential element of the rustic setting, and many people have found creative solutions to the problem. Antler chandeliers look great when hung over the dining-room table. Antique antler lighting is, however, very expensive and difficult to find. New antler lighting is available in all shapes and sizes from many companies around the country. Or try making an antler chandelier yourself; it's not as difficult as you may think. You do have to be very careful when electrifying your fixture. It is best to call an electrician for assistance.

Many people choose less-expensive lighting and have turned to chandeliers made from old lanterns, wagon wheels, used hubcaps, antique canoe paddles and oars, and all sorts of other inventive materials. These folk-art creations can be really wonderful, especially when dramatic lamp shades are used. One individual assembled a stunning chandelier from his childhood canoe paddles and six Tiffany art-glass shades. Other artistic people have constructed lamps from a mass of twigs woven together, drift-

LEFT The dining room at the Eddy Chalet was full of cedar furniture which was quite comfortable and built to last for many seasons.

wood, birchbark, cedar logs and hollowed-out trees.

I have seen dining tables and other areas of rustic homes lit with leaded-glass chandeliers made by the Tiffany Company and other firms. The effects of such lighting are usually stunning. If the originals are too expensive, reproductions of these lamps are available throughout the country. Be sure to have the lamps installed by a qualified electrician. An ounce of prevention is worth a ton of cures.

DECORATIVE ACCESSORIES

Decorating your dining-room table is very important. Rustic centerpieces are always interesting, and it is intriguing to see how different people use them. Often seen are

bowls made from the hollowed-out burls of trees. Many creative craftspeople have also constructed unique centerpieces out of roots, sticks and antlers that hold glasses, bottles, knives or candles.

Place mats can add color and depth to a dining room. Small Indian weavings make beautiful place mats, as do woven reeds or splints. Dark green, brown and red mats enrich a table. Silverware with handles made from small twigs and branches is presently on the market, and antique carving sets adorned with antler handles are available at antique shops and flea markets.

Salt and pepper shakers are now also being made of both twigs and hollowed-out antlers. Furthermore, contemporary dishes are available

with all sorts of rustic motifs, including log cabins, moose and deer silhouettes, and fishing and hunting scenes. Old dishes and place settings occasionally become available when a camp or lodge goes out of business and the contents are sold at auction. These auctions are great places to find all sorts of items that enhance the ambience of the rustic setting.

No matter how many colorful and clever furnishings and accessories you may have, the heart of a really great rustic dining room is people. Have your friends and family over often, enjoy a great meal together, and get to know each other.

ABOVE   Contemporary bureau showing a significant Eastlake influence, is decorated with both
the inner and outer layer of birchbark exposed.
Bureaus are sometimes used in dining rooms for
storing table linens and flatware.

ABOVE   Sideboard by Reverend Ben Davis, built around 1920. Attention to detail and form make Davis's pieces highly covetable.

ABOVE Round table and armchairs serve as a
casual breakfast spot to watch the sunrise over
Lake George in the Adirondacks. Mellow wainscot
siding throughout the house adds a sense of
warmth on cool mountain days.

ABOVE   An antique rustic rocking chair and green root table fit well into the classic country setting. The chair is constructed of magnolia branches and was found in North Carolina.

E. L. GOODYKOONTZ

A blacksmith by trade, E. L. Goodykoontz was a bachelor of German descent who lived with his sister. His shop was in Sweet Springs, Virginia. ❦ Goodykoontz was a big man, over six feet tall. According to his nephew, he was not a well-liked individual; his gruffness and bluntness made him unpopular in the community. ❦ As a furniture maker, he is known for his classic designs. He made his own large rose-head nails and spent many hours gathering materials for chairs and settees. Gathering in the Appalachian Mountains apparently was not an easy task: Goodykoontz and others spent more time killing snakes than actually gathering wood. ❦ Construction of the chairs and settees took about two to three days each. Goodykoontz also made hall trees and porch swings. For chairs and rockers, he charged $1.25, and the charge for a settee was $5.00. One feature that makes a Goodykoontz piece identifiable is that the bar running across the top and joining the two back posts is straight, unlike those of other builders, who frequently used curved sticks in the back post. Goodykoontz also frequently inlaid the seats of his chair. ❦ Goodykoontz was obviously quite fond of the naturalness of the building materials. One settee has golf balls embedded in the heavy burled sections on the end of the arms. Other pieces have arms with gnarls that have almost completely grown around rocks. He left the rocks in place and used the wood as he found it. ❦ His style shows Gothic influences, and he incorporated a Chinese Chippendale motif in the backs of chairs and settees. He was most active in the furniture business between 1900 and 1920. He died at age ninety-three.

ABOVE Root rocker by E. L. Goodykoontz in a country setting of masonry and cherry corner cupboards.

ABOVE   Contemporary table and picture
frame by Judd Weisberg surrounds an antique
deer painting from the 1920s.

ABOVE   This oriental root set, in original finish, is eighteenth-century and probably from Japan. The seats were once cushioned with red velvet. The Victorian swag lamp and the mirror of scrub pine make nice accents. (Photo © 1993 by George Bouret)

ABOVE A root armchair fits comfortably into a traditional country setting of folk and tramp art, kitchen collectibles, baskets and oriental rugs.

ABOVE Contemporary kitchen cupboard by Clifford
Monteith is the home for this collection of antique
Dedham pottery. The cupboard is constructed of young
willow shoots.

A B O V E This Maine summer house is a marvel of high technology and subtle rustic decor. The dining table is by Gustav Stickley and contemporary chairs are by Barry Gregson. Antique candle sticks are by Jarvie.

A B O V E   Antique Old Hickory drop-leaf, gate-leg table and chairs by L. A. Simmons of Bedford, Indiana, ca. 1930s. The china cabinet is by Reverend Ben Davis and the shelf unit is from the Appalachian region. The house overlooks a cypress-lined lake in Florida.

ABOVE   This eighteenth-century cupboard was found in Czechoslovakia. The construction of the piece is generally superior to that of similar American pieces. The drawers are dovetailed and the mosaic twig work is intricately placed throughout. The top is detachable and the crest reads "KM" with a six-pointed star.

A B O V E Sideboard by Ernest Stowe of the upper Saranac Lake region of the Adirondacks.
The piece was constructed in 1904 and presently is privately housed in the Adirondacks.

RIGHT These antique hickory chairs have been recovered with material from old Indian-pattern blankets. The metal "fruit" lamp offers a continued natural method to light areas. Oriental rugs throughout the house bring drama to the rustic with their natural colors and patterns.

BOTTOM This is the most dramatic antique Old Hickory dining-room set known today. The table expands to seat ten people, who can watch the sun set over a beautiful lake in the Adirondacks. The weaving on the chairs, table and sideboard is extremely rare. The set is in perfect condition.

ABOVE & LEFT Dining-room suite and
side chair by Reverend Ben Davis. The twelve-
piece set offers high drama in the Victorian setting where it presently resides in North
Carolina. Davis was known for his superb
attention to details and design. The set was
completed in the 1920s.

ABOVE The rustic dining table is constructed of massive rhododendron branches that have been chip-carved. The tabletop is quarter-sawn oak. The table was found in a North Carolina department store, and, although it is not clear who made the table, it is in the style of the locale where it was found. The Windsor chairs were made by the Old Hickory Company in the 1930s, and the antler chandelier and wall sconces are from the Black Forest.

RUSTIC BEDROOMS

Bedrooms are the most personal

rooms in our homes. They are profound statements

about the individuals who reside there. They are rooms

for quiet times and intimacy. Bedrooms are so trusted

that we allow ourselves to become unconscious in them.

They hold our most personal belongings, and we go to

The most extreme and wild rustic beds are made out of huge limbs and adorned with all the wild branches, twigs, buds and nests that they maintained in the wild.

them to be rejuvenated and refreshed. Bedrooms in the rustic style are havens from the outside world. They are places of longing and fantasy that bring us closer to nature.

Often rustic furniture makers are influenced not only by their imagination, but by the forms inherent in the woods available to them. Consequently, rustic furniture has an attitude of ruggedness, independence and individuality that is similar to that of the builders who create it. At the same time, there is something wonderfully romantic about going out in your backyard and cutting materials to be used for your furniture, especially something as intimate as your bedroom set.

BEDS

Beds used in rustic homes range from the absolutely simple and "shakerist" in style, to imposing and gargantuan in size. Four-poster beds are constructed of hickory, birch, cedar or other woods that are accessible to the builder. Craftspeople have expanded the design to make head and footboards that mimic mission and prairie-school patterns or are decorated with other naturally occurring geometric patterns. The most extreme and wild rustic beds are made out of huge limbs and adorned with all the wild

branches, twigs, buds and nests that they maintained in the wild.

Rustic beds, like beds everywhere, come in all shapes and sizes. Craftspeople today are creating king- and queen-size beds, bed frames for water beds, bunk beds, beds with canopies and numerous other variations dictated by personal needs. One very creative individual transformed live tree branches into bed frames for a child's tree house.

BUREAUS, CHAIRS & TABLES

Although beds are the principle focus in bedrooms, other furnishings add balance and livability. Comfortable bedrooms have places to throw and hang our clothes, a spot for the cat to sleep and some form of lighting to help us find lost things.

Bureaus made of birchbark and twigs continue the rustic design in the bedroom. Many people, however, choose antique country-pine cottage chests as alternatives to pieces made of bark and sticks. Others select furniture by Stickley, Limbert and other mission designers. These second styles are philosophically consistent with that of rustic furniture, and the individual pieces work well together.

Twig rocking chairs made by the Amish are incredibly comfortable and quite functional. Old and new chairs by the Old Hickory Furniture Company last forever and can be upholstered to match any color scheme.

Rustic tables are welcome additions to any bedroom and are ideal places for table lamps, mirrors, clocks and other necessities. Table lamps made of twigs, branches, antlers or hooves are striking.

These lamps can be covered with parchment shades that produce a warm glow and greatly enhance the ambience of the rustic setting.

BED COVERINGS & ACCESSORIES

Linens and bed coverings selected for bedrooms tend to be in bold earth tones and patterns indicative of nature. Hudson Bay, Pendleton, Earlys and others manufacture colorful, heavy wool blankets that add drama to any room. Cotton and flannel sheets in bright "north woods" designs (e.g., hunting-jacket patterns) and deep tones of rich greens and browns make sleep warm and restful. Blankets, robes and pajamas of cowboy and Indian designs by the Pendleton company and others extend the

ABOVE This daybed is part of a rustic set from the Lake Rabun Hotel in Georgia. The set was made in the 1920s and 1930s.

ABOVE   The antique hickory vanity is ideal for this young girl's room in New York.

RIGHT   Probably the most dramatic driftwood rustic bed ever made, this one was constructed by Judd Weisberg in 1984. The bed presently resides in Connecticut.

rustic motif even further. Throw pillows created from antique oriental rugs, blankets and linens add the finishing touches to a rustic bedroom. A handmade antique quilt contributes a special human touch to the room where we spend one-third of our lives.

Bedrooms are also home to intimate collections of personal memorabilia. Gifts from our families, photos of past generations, and small collectible souvenirs often grace the tops of bureaus, bookcases or vanities. Photos, certificates and letters

hang on walls in old frames made of bark, twigs and antlers. Small collectible boxes made of similar materials provide storage places for jewelry, perfume or other intimate items. Hand-held mirrors, hair-brushes and combs which are constructed of antlers or have log handles bring the presence of the wilderness into the bedroom setting.

In short, bedrooms are places to experience both wild dreams and rejuvenating rest. Sleep well and safely in the arms of nature.

ABOVE The root settee and twig chair fit nicely into this English-style bedroom. The settee was originally found in Delaware.

RIGHT The four-poster bed by The Rustic Hickory Furniture Company feels natural in this log home. Antique quilts give the room a personal touch.

ABOVE   The swirls of the twig rocking chair are classically Southern. The colors from the hanging textiles

blend naturally with the walls and furniture in this Georgia lakeside home.

ABOVE Clifford Monteith created this queen-size bed. The deer-hoof lamps were made in the 1930s.

ABOVE Exquisite antique twig chairs are from North Carolina. The antique lamps are adorned with mica shades which cast mellow hues throughout the room.

ABOVE   Rhododendron root settee made by E. L. Goodykoontz around 1910 in the springs area of Virginia. The large root knots at the end of each arm hold an embedded golf ball.

ABOVE   The chaise lounge and poster bed were made by the Rustic Hickory Furniture Company around 1910.

RIGHT   A stunning bureau and mirror by Clifford Monteith. The reflection in the mirror shows an antique Gustav Stickley china cabinet. A collection of birchbark items graces the top of the bureau.

A B O V E Birch bureau with mirror by Ernest Stowe, upper Saranac Lake, New York, ca. 1905. It is one of only two known bureaus by Stowe, who is considered the consummate rustic furniture builder of the Adirondacks. He retired to Florida about 1911, and occasionally a piece or two of his surfaces in that area.

A B O V E   This bedroom setting is actually in the back of a New Hampshire fisherman's garage. The
massive armchair is from the Adirondacks, and the new birch bed was made by Lionel Maurier.

A B O V E   Brent McGregor, a builder in Oregon, constructed this massive contemporary bed out of lodgepole pines. The simple lines and form of the bed are made infinitely more intricate by the natural contours, color, and variations within the wood itself.

A B O V E A wicker and sweet-grass desk set blend nicely with the
Southern rocker. Green drapes add richness throughout the house.

TOP Bunk beds are ideal for this small bedroom at a lakeside house in Maine. The bureau was designed by Harvey Ellis and built by Gustav Stickley around 1903.

BOTTOM The antique yellow birch rocker is from the early part of this century, made in the Adirondacks. The hickory desk was made by Old Hickory around 1925, as was the hickory lamp.

ABOVE   Birchbark vanity made by "Injun Joe" in the 1920s in the North Woods of Maine. The piece
fits nicely under the eaves of this New Hampshire log home.

RUSTIC PORCHES

OPPOSITE   A weathered Indiana hickory hoop chair on the porch of a log home in South Carolina has provided seventy years of rest for its owner.

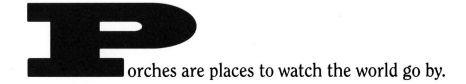orches are places to watch the world go by.

They are the ideal spot to meet and greet neighbors, family

and friends. They are locations for play on rainy days, cat-

naps, and quiet conversations. Porches were so important

to the Victorians that their tongue-in-cheek rationale

was to "build the porch first and add the house later."

Traditional rustic porches are places to repair an outboard motor, work on fishing gear, enjoy a favorite beverage and commiserate with others over the "one that got away." More-formal rustic porches are homes to fascinating plants, exotic birds, whirlpool baths, and Sunday brunches and aperitifs. Rest and relaxation, however, are the uses that all good porches have in common.

Some porches are large enough for cookouts and picnic tables, which means that they often serve as sites for championship checkers matches, poker games, and various forms of artistic endeavor. In the natural realm, porches are havens for all sorts of potted and hanging plants that need shelter from the elements. Porches may also harbor several bird feeders, dog bowls, and beds for pets in need of rest.

Many rustic porches are constructed of cedar logs, fieldstone, driftwood, or other natural materials. A creative individual will make sure that the woods used in construction retain their original twists, contortions and connecting appendages. These natural materials frequently form the railings and banisters of porches as well as their frames. Using materials this way allows a builder to capture the ambience and atmosphere of the wilderness. When coming from the outdoors and preparing to enter the house, the porch is a good buffer, maintaining a significant feeling of continuity with the outdoors.

PORCH FURNITURE

Furniture for the porch should be a combination of "rugged" and "comfortable." Armchairs have to withstand the torment and indignity of having their back legs leaned upon for hours at a time. Coffee tables should be sturdy enough to tolerate an onslaught of shoes, boots, and beverage containers. Settees, gliders, and porch swings should be able to survive endless nappers, guitar players, visiting cousins, and thankful mailpersons. Rocking chairs, synonymous with rest and relaxation, need to be comfortable, but also capable of withstanding years of abuse and neglect.

The types of furniture most often used on rustic porches include Indiana hickory, mission, Amish twig, willow, wicker, cedar, Kennedy rockers, and Westport chairs. Most porches actually combine all these types.

Also occasionally seen on porches in the resort areas of the East and South are massive settees, chairs, rockers, and tables made of rhododendron roots and other twisted materials. These huge pieces are known primarily for their aesthetic and rugged appeal and definitely not for their comfort. One well-known person who enjoyed his privacy had chairs made from roots on his porch for a specific reason: guests could only tolerate sitting in them for fifteen minutes and usually left after a brief visit.

Porch furniture cannot be left uncared-for. Rustic furnishings are nothing more than organic material. Consequently, exposure to the elements and moisture of any kind will accelerate decomposition, regardless of how much paint or polyurethane is applied. So remember to keep your porch furniture dry and away from direct sunlight. If properly protected from the weather, porch furniture can last for decades and serve your interests for people-watching.

The types of furniture most often used on rustic porches include Indiana hickory, mission, Amish twig, willow, wicker, cedar, Kennedy rockers, and Westport chairs.

ABOVE A dramatic Southern twig chair thought
to be made by the gypsies in the Appalachians
during the early part of this century.

ABOVE This is one of the most unique folk-art rustic chairs in existence. The heads were carved out of the roots of the branches that were used as the structure for the piece, ca. 1950.

ABOVE A massive settee and matching chair are ideal for this front porch. It is interesting to note the Mission influence in the two pieces. Gustav Stickley was making very similar spindle furniture at the same time this set was constructed (1902).

TOP   These paddle armchairs overlook Lake George in the Adirondacks. They were made by the Westport Chair Company, which operated between 1904 and 1930 in Westport, New York.

RIGHT   Exterior view of a Maine lake-house porch. The porch blends superbly with piles of driftwood that wash up on the shores.

ABOVE This solitary, prison-made Indiana hickory chair offers a moment of rest for those visiting the front porch of this Southern log home. The prisoners made thousands of these chairs during the thirties and forties, and the chairs furnished many of the public buildings in Indiana.

A B O V E A contemporary settee overlooks a pond in New Jersey.

A B O V E   This settee, made from the branches of apple trees, presently resides in an apple orchard from where the materials originally came. The settee is a favorite resting place for cross-country skiers during the long New Hampshire winters.

A B O V E   The intricate patterns in this Victorian root settee were apparently influenced by early works from China and Japan. This piece was found in the basement of a Rhode Island apartment building and was moved to New Hampshire.

L E F T   The gardens in Vancouver have many pergolas, trellises, gazebos and other natural ornamentations. Strolling in this environment is just like walking in the woods.

A B O V E   Woodpeckers have been seen pecking away at this furniture in the early morning in hopes of a meal, but in the afternoon the cedar gypsy lounge chairs are perfect for relaxing.

ABOVE A pair of oversized Old Hickory armchairs serve as a site for an afternoon of bird watching in New Hampshire.

A B O V E Joe Quinn, of Virginia, built this root rocker around the turn of the century. His construction techniques, chip carving, and use of symmetry distinguish his work among rustic builders.

JOSEPH CLARENCE QUINN

J oseph Clarence Quinn was born on June 20, 1882, the oldest of eight children. According to Quinn's son, he was a barber by profession. During much of his life, he was also a caretaker at the resort Greenbriar in White Sulphur Springs, Virginia. ❦ *He lived at the foot of Kate Mountain in a small cabin that he lined with roots. Like Goodykoontz, whom he knew and worked with for a short time, Quinn built rustic furniture out of the massive rhododendron bushes that covered the mountain directly behind his house. His pieces, however, were not as massive as were Goodykoontz's. Instead, he made scaled-down versions and chip-carved the many tables, swings, settees, rockers and other items that he produced. He often removed all the bark from the branches before building the furniture. He was also known to split large branches in half and use both sides in construction.* ❦ *Fees for Quinn's furniture were average for that time—$5.00 for a settee, $3.00 for a child's toy set, and $1.25 for a rocker.* ❦ *Quinn stopped building in 1940 and died in 1973.*

ABOVE This dock, built by Clifford Monteith, reaches into the lake and seems to be nothing more than an extension of the woods that surround the area.

ABOVE The porch and furniture were built by Clifford Monteith in Michigan and assembled at this site in Maine.
The heavy use of peeled cedar sticks adds significant intensity to the setting. The contemporary Arts and Crafts chandelier,
made of hammered copper, is by Michael Adams.

ABOVE The Chinese Chippendale influence is evident in the forms of many root chairs such as these, which were made in North Carolina and now serve as a rustic retreat on a porch in New England.

RIGHT Walking along the edge of the reservoir just south of Asheville, North Carolina, one stumbles on this huge sculpture of two bears hugging. There is no obvious reason for its being in this location, but the artistic rendition of the animals, cut from a single tree, is superb.

A B O V E   This set from the Lake Rabun Hotel bears a striking resemblance to pieces made by Kenny Runion, who lived very close to the hotel and was working with this material in the same time period as the hotel furniture was built—the 1930s.

ABOVE   Part of the Lake Rabun Hotel set,
these two antique pieces are situated so guests
can have a quiet afternoon snack on the patio.

A B O V E   This Florida setting is a favorite place to watch the sun go down and see the alligators swim by.

ABOVE   A traditional Southern log cabin porch is ideal for this painted Old Hickory settee. The Indian blanket warms people on cold evenings.

WALLS, WINDOWS, FLOORS AND DOORS

ustic decor and furnishings

have been utilized in almost every conceivable living situ-

ation devised by the human race. However, only certain

types of walls, windows, floors and doors are consistent

with the rustic philosophy of simplicity, and working

with and enhancing the environment and nature.

OPPOSITE Windows trimmed in apple-tree wood certainly add an outdoorsy touch to the starkness of plain walls.

WALLS

Materials and designs frequently used on walls when decorating in the rustic style include logs, wainscoting, barn board (knotty pine), white plasterboard, post and beam with white plasterboards, or fieldstone. Less often seen in rustic homes are wallpaper, stucco, textured surfaces, mirrors, or high-tech wall coverings.

The most popular choices are log or wainscoted walls. Log homes have come a long way since their inception many years ago. Log homes today are marvels of high technology, yet consistently retain their rustic flavor. However, many decorators and designers, wishing to use the rustic style only partially, may select log walls for just one room. This is easily accomplished by nailing log siding directly into the wall studs.

Wainscoting is also frequently utilized on both walls and ceilings. Developed during the Victorian period, wainscoting greatly enhances rustic flavor because of natural wood's warm ambience and mellow patina. Wainscoted boards have a small groove cut into their length. When assembled, they produce a dramatic texturing and sense of movement. Hundreds of upwardly mobile lines awaken a spiritual presence and add a sense of mystery to any room. The boards are frequently made of soft woods and darken dramatically with age.

Barn boards are also an attractive material to finish a room. Old barn boards are available at many architectural salvage yards, or rough-cut (knotty pine) lumber can be purchased at a lumberyard. Many decorators use large rosehead or square-cut nails to secure these boards to the walls, thus adding to the rugged effect.

White plasterboard walls are also frequently seen in rustic settings. Their ease to both maintain and adapt makes white walls a favorite with decorators. Their strength, of course, is that white backgrounds accentuate any decorative item placed on them.

Post-and-beam settings combine the rustic appeal of logs and plasterboard. Like log homes, post-and-beam houses today are both high-tech and user friendly. One distinctive advantage of logs and of post-and-beam settings is that nails for hanging decorative accessories can be driven and removed with little concern for the marks or impressions they leave. Often the more distressed a log or board looks, the better.

Another desirable material for home or porch construction is fieldstone. These stones make a surprisingly positive contribution to the

Stones make a surprisingly positive contribution to the rustic feel of a home's interior.

rustic feel of a home's interior. In reality, stones are as natural to the earth as trees and wind. Two distinct disadvantages are, however, the difficulty in placing a nail in them for hanging one's favorite painting, and, less obvious, the continual problem with dust accumulation. These two considerations aside, homes with rocks in them last forever, are easy to heat and are naturally beautiful.

WINDOWS

Window treatments in the rustic setting consistently range between minimalist and nonexistent. It is surprising how many decorators use little or no treatment on rustic windows. The effect is still impressive. Why interfere with the beautiful outdoor scenery?

Some decorators, however, have been quite creative in the treatment of rustic windows. Occasionally, individuals will cut up old Pendleton or Indian blankets or Kilim rugs and create not only great curtains, but pillows, throw rugs, and other decorative accessories as well. Others have used striped-ticking cotton material, not unlike that found in mattresses, to make very attractive curtains. Nonetheless, rustic settings seem to be enhanced by minimum treatment of windows.

Entranceways to the rustic home are dramatically enhanced by large, antique Victorian doors or custom-made rustic doors.

Another option is to trim the interior side of the windows with logs that have been split in half. The effects of this treatment are quite dramatic. Windows trimmed this way are left without curtains and the headaches of maintaining them.

FLOORS

Floors, on the other hand, are treated more elaborately. Natural wood flooring of oak, maple or pine boards looks beautiful and rugged. Or thick wall-to-wall carpeting, in light tan, beige or brown, often accentuates the furniture placed on it.

On the other hand, many people select oriental rugs for their rustic homes. Rugs with rich browns and reds, such as Herizes, Kashans, Kilims, and others, definitely add richness and character to a room. Indian rugs made by the Navajos and other tribes contribute a sense of naturalness, boldness, and courage to the setting.

Folk rugs are another choice for a rustic home. Folk rugs from the Grenfell Industries in Canada, Penny rugs from New England, and a wide variety of hooked rugs from throughout the country add personality to the walls and floors of a home.

Less suited for a rustic setting are Chinese rugs, which are used more successfully with formal decor.

DOORS

Entranceways to the rustic home are dramatically enhanced by large, antique Victorian doors or custom-made rustic doors. Nothing beats the strength and security of an antique oak door, which can often be found at a salvage yard. Try to find one that has beveled-glass or stained-glass windows.

Another possibility is to have a local craftsperson construct a door from logs cut on your own property. This is a great way to blend your home with its natural surroundings and make a statement of originality. If you have a really talented wood carver in your neighborhood, you may want to have the interior of the door frame trimmed with a carved replica of logs, complete with birch nests or other things normally found in trees.

Once again, don't be afraid to experiment with your house. Be creative. If you run out of ideas, go for a walk in the woods and see what colors predominate in your area. Then bring those colors inside your home.

RIGHT The framing around the door is hand carved to resemble the lines of nature. Take note of the rabbit in the lower right-hand corner.

ABOVE Rustic frames become the artwork themselves. The middle birch frame is by Ernest Stowe and the root table was found in an apartment building in Washington, D.C.

A B O V E The stairway in this log cabin is surrounded by taxidermy and other rustic accessories. The small table is by Reverend Ben Davis.

A B O V E   The chip-carved rhododendron root table has a single-board top of chestnut. A collection of birchbark frames and canoes and an antique log cabin are the focal points of this living room. The table was found at a flea market in Pennsylvania. The setting is illuminated by antique Old Hickory floor lamps with mica shades.

ABOVE Rustic colors are presented in a variety of textiles from the 1920s and 1930s. Many companies were making fabrics that evoked the spirit of outdoors, including Hudson Bay, Pendleton, Montgomery Ward, and others.

ABOVE   The owner of this home in New Hampshire is a designer by trade and a part-time musician who likes to have an audience at his concerts. The antique and contemporary decoys that occupy every corner of the home fill the house with a profound sense of nature.

ABOVE Tourist-trade artwork is very collectible, inexpensive, and available. It often adds a needed and interesting touch to vacant spaces, as it does here at the entrance to the restroom.

ABOVE A nook under the eaves of a log cabin is decorated with interesting tables, a root lamp, and several birch tourist-trade accessories.

LEFT The hall tree and matching grandfather clock were made by a New England farmer and part-time carpenter and school teacher. The pieces are constructed of apple-tree wood and are signed "H. Wright, January 26, 1901, Lexington, Massachusetts."

ABOVE Cottage-pine furniture works quite well in the rustic

setting. Painted creels and pack baskets also add to the ambience.

ABOVE High-end creel collection and a rustic hickory bed are enhanced by the green saw-tooth quilt. Creels are receiving a considerable amount of attention today as works of art. It took several seasons to collect the antique creels shown here.

ABOVE Cowboy, Indian, and rustic items blend perfectly together, evoking the spirituality of the wild. This kind of combination works as well in a Manhattan apartment as in a rustic mountain retreat.

LEFT The doorway to the bedroom is framed in cedar logs. Linear lines, such as pictured here, show the influence of oriental and prairie-school designs.

ABOVE The entrance to this home in Georgia is decorated with antique toy furniture from the Old
Hickory Furniture Company. The toys were produced by the thousands and have become collectibles.

RUSTIC ACCESSORIES

alking into a room decorated

with rustic furniture and accessories evokes feelings

that most of us welcome. In many of our homes today,

we are surrounded by the evidence of high technology,

including televisions and stereo equipment, microwaves,

and other modern appliances that leave us feeling cold,

OPPOSITE The root plant stand makes an ideal table for the log cabin which was made in the Appalachian area in the early part of the century. Log cabins such as the one here frequently had lights inside and were used as holiday decorations.

LEFT Contemporary clock by Jerry and Jessica Farrell. Jerry does the woodwork and his wife, Jessica, creates individual paintings for their rustic furnishings.

oppressed, and overly restricted. A room full of rustic, however, inspires feelings of warmth, comfort and a closeness to nature. Rustic environments invite us to relax, take off our shoes, and feel as if we are in the woods and part of the natural world. A stone fireplace, a log cabin, Indian rugs, taxidermy, tables made from roots, sweeping willow chairs, photos and paintings, signs, and a couch made of cedar and upholstered with Indian blankets all capture the colors of the earth.

Walk through the woods and see what colors speak to you: greens, browns, reds; different intensities, different hues. They all seem to work together. Even bright flowers and other dramatic colors appear to blend perfectly. What you see outside should be brought inside. Look out the windows of your house and what do you see? Bring these colors and forms inside and your home will become a continuous extension of the outdoors.

The shapes of rustic furniture

are full of movement and fun. They contain huge amounts of humor and rebellion. Forms in nature are free to follow their own calling. Yes, they have been influenced by other forces in their own environment, but for the most part, they do what they want. It is that freedom that calls to us. Forget about the boss and the mortgage; let freedom inside and be yourself for a while.

One of the nicest things about decorating in the rustic style is that accessories are readily available, as

LEFT Throw pillows made from antique Navajo rugs provide color and comfort for rustic settings.

well as inexpensive. Although it is true that many of the really great North Woods and root pieces can be quite costly and are almost impossible to find, for the most part you can, if you are creative, tenacious, and lucky, decorate an entire room (or house, for that matter) for very little money.

Many decorative rustic accessories are available at flea markets, junk shops, and yard sales, as well as through antique dealers and at auctions and antique shows. Old signs that advertise COTTAGES FOR RENT, NO FISHING OR HUNTING, BAIT SHOPS and RESORTS, or directions to lakes and lodges are wonderful as wall hangings. The more colorful the better. Earlier signs were painted on wood, while later ones were lettered on tin and occasionally on glass.

A note of caution and a rule always to follow: ask the person who is selling it if the piece is old or new. Everything ever made is being reproduced today, including old rustic signs and advertising. Some unscrupulous individuals may try to sell you a brand new sign that looks old for the higher price of an antique. Don't be taken in; learn to recognize the difference between old and new.

SPORTS EQUIPMENT

Snowshoes, old wooden-tipped skis, old tie-up ski boots and bamboo ski poles look great in corners and on walls. Wooden skis were produced by many different companies and often can be found with

the original decals depicting their makers and origins. Occasionally, ski poles were painted or had a red plastic finish on them. If they are colorful, so much the better. Old snowshoes were made in several different styles. The long snowshoes are referred to as Michigans or pickerels and were intended for long, open field hikes. Snowshoes that are very wide are called bear paws, for obvious reasons, and were used for hiking in the dense woods.

Snowshoes were made by several different commercial companies, as well as individually by the Indians in many different parts of the country. Indian snowshoes are considerably more desirable, as they were handmade and usually display finer detail, including small tufts of wool on the fronts of the shoes, very fine weaving, and other embellishments.

Fishing memorabilia is also very decorative. Old wooden and bamboo rods with fishing reels look great on walls. Fishing creels in their many different forms work well in collections and also serve as holders for plants and dried flowers. Fishing nets are also fun decorations. Use either the small hand-held trout nets or the longer salmon nets as accessories in any way your imagination suggests. Old lures, reels, flies, and other small items are nice touches, but because of their sizes they are difficult to display except in a case. Old basket packs are also wonderful and can be left on floors, hung on walls, or used in any number of creative ways.

Old trophies also make great decorative items. They come in all shapes and sizes and are made of sterling silver, silver plate, bronze, or copper wash. Obviously, the sterling ones are going to be signifi-

cantly more expensive, but trophies made of alternative materials are equally as decorative and much more affordable. Trophies are inscribed from all sorts of organizations for many different activities, including fishing, road racing, sailing, and as awards for best salesman and best rooster, among other things. Collectors should also be aware that some trophy themes are much more desirable than others. For instance, sailing and golf trophies are very popular, while those connected with activities such as wrestling or billiards may not be as highly sought after. The general rule is: the more desirable, the more expensive the trophy.

Many collectors spend a significant amount of time polishing their trophies so they look like new. Frankly, polished items can look *too* new. If you want an authentic rus-

RIGHT Child's Indiana hickory settee and a group of birchbark picture frames and boxes.

tic look, avoid overpolishing and keep the mellow patina that took years to develop. Also avoid trophies that are excessively dented, because these unwanted creases are very difficult to remove. When buying silver-plate trophies, make sure that the silver has not completely worn away and left the piece very dark looking.

OLD PHOTOGRAPHS

One of the great undiscovered art treasures of the world is old photographs. Photos of people fishing, skiing, camping, sailing, rocking on porches, or involved in other recreational pursuits are available to those willing to seek them out. Photos of sports teams are also very decorative. Nature photographs depicting rivers, mountains, lakes and streams, sunsets, clouds, and other outdoor wonders can be striking, too.

When buying old photos, only collect those that are aesthetically pleasing to you. Make sure they are in excellent condition with no stains or tears. When possible, get them in frames, or collect old frames and use them with unframed photos. Be aware that many old photos are being reproduced. Always ask the dealer if a particular photo is new or old so you can be aware of its monetary value.

BIRDHOUSES AND LOG CABINS

Old birdhouses and toy log cabins also make wonderful decorations. Birdhouses look great in their original bright paint, but be sure to wash them off as they may contain microbes left over from past residents. Miniature log cabins were made by all sorts of folk artists, as well as Boy Scouts and as projects in woodworking classes.

Many of these small cabins are filled with rustic furniture or may have been intended as mailboxes or have lights on the inside. (Common sense tells us to have the electrified cabins rewired before we plug them in.) Other old rustic items in this genre include early Lincoln log-home construction sets. I must admit that I own several of these and have spent many "lazy" hours constructing my own rustic log compounds.

BOATS AND BOATING EQUIPMENT

Old boats make wonderful ceiling hangers, modified cupboards, and coffee tables. Early boats, including canoes, guide boats, rowboats, and kayaks, look impressive hanging from the ceiling. The most desirable are those that are ribbed in the interior. Full-size birchbark canoes look great but can be very

expensive and difficult to locate. Several canoe companies that made wood and canvas boats existed in the 1920s and 1930s, including Old Town and others. Old Town canoes always featured diamond fasteners on the gunnels and were usually signed with a decal on either the bow or stern splashboards. Old ship and pond models also make excellent props and certainly add an air of freedom and a touch of beauty to any room.

Old sailboats, however, are a bit tricky. The difficulty lies in transporting them after their purchase. They are usually very fragile and must be handled with the greatest of care. If they should be broken, however, it is not difficult to repair them. Match the color of the thread used in the rigging and new sails can be sewn out of muslin.

(Remember to stain the new sails with strong tea before rigging them, as tea will make them look quite old.) If a mast is broken, it can be repaired using an old dole rod purchased from the local lumber store. Remember to stain the rod before reconnecting it to the rigging on the boat.

If you are going to hang one of these beautiful boats, make sure you do a thorough job so the boat won't come crashing down on you at some unexpected moment. Also don't hesitate to buy an old boat that has had the canvas removed. A simple coat of varnish or other finishing product will return color to the wood, and it is not necessary to recanvas an old boat in order to use it for decorative purposes.

Along with the old boats, don't forget to use old canoe paddles and

oars as decorative props. Paddles often have colorful designs painted on them and are frequently decorated with camp insignias identifying where they came from. One may also find oars that still have the old brass or steel oar locks on them. Old double-bladed or kayak paddles also make interesting decorations and look wonderful hanging from walls and ceilings. Rowboat oars can also be used successfully. If you are really lucky, you may also find a pair of old skulling or curved oars used by rowing teams. Occasionally these oars are adorned with the names of the team members, schools, competitions, or other colorful designs. Also try to find oars that still have the leather wrappings or oarlocks on them. These add to the originality and look great.

Sailing memorabilia can also be

RIGHT Antique fishing bobbers, although small, are great little rustic collectibles. The colors and forms of the many different types of bobbers make collecting and displaying them an interesting pastime.

used creatively when decorating a rustic room. Photos of the great lodges and hotels in the Adirondacks frequently show canoes and small sailing boats on the many lakes of that region. Old Adirondack guide-boat seats, life vests, telescopes and binoculars, and a wide variety of other sailing equipment can add charm and color to any number of room arrangements.

Miniature canoes and boats are also very collectible and decorative. The Indians made thousands of them to be sold to tourists in many areas around the country. These boats were either hand-carved from tree branches or made of birchbark. Handmade birch canoes are considered very desirable, and the hand-sewn, intricate ones command hundreds of dollars at sales. Other less intricate miniature canoes are

significantly cheaper, and for the rustic home, equally as decorative.

It should also be mentioned that miniature paddles are great accessories, especially when presented on a white wall or other area where they will stand out. Some paddles were sold as souvenirs and may have scenes depicting Indians or rustic settings. They frequently bear the name of the place where they were purchased, such as the Catskills, Adirondacks, or other resort area.

MINIATURES

On the subject of miniatures, it is intriguing that almost every company produced either salesman samples or child-sized replicas of the actual items they were selling. These miniatures make wonderful decorations. The Old Hickory Company in Indiana made toy-size

doll furniture. The Old Town Canoe Company made salesman samples of their canoes. Lund Skis made miniature skis. Paris Snowshoes made miniature snowshoes. Other companies made tiny fishing creels, basket packs, canoe paddles and numerous other "little treasures." Collecting "smalls" is a great pastime, and these little accessories add a lot of charm to a rustic setting.

DUCK DECOYS

Certainly one of the most decorative rustic items available is duck decoys. Decoys were made in every state in the country, and the best ones—those with great paint and wonderful symmetry—are highly collectible. It is not unusual to see one of these prize ducks bring many thousands of dollars at auction. Nonetheless, good decoys that most

ABOVE The extraordinary apple-tree grand-father clock was made in 1901 in Lexington, Massachusetts, by Mr. H. Wright, a local carpenter, teacher and farmer. He also built a hall tree pictured in this book and a stunning twelve-foot, stump-based dining table.

of us can afford are available at almost every antique show or flea market.

Keep in mind that the better the likeness and paint, the more valuable the duck is. Avoid decoys that are full of shotgun holes, and if you're paying the price for an old one, make sure that the duck is truly old. New decoys are being manufactured today by the thousands and are very inexpensive.

TAXIDERMY ITEMS

Almost every rustic room ever decorated has at least some taxidermy. During the past few years, this has become a controversial issue as populations of rare animals continue to decline. Realistically, the hunting of animals for food has been going on for a long time and will not stop. In my opinion, it is acceptable to shoot something if the sole intention is to eat it. However, very few people eat lions, tigers, elephants, seals, doves, birds of prey, or numerous other animals. It is unethical to destroy them. They have a right to be here, and we have a responsibility to ensure their survival.

You should be aware that there are laws that prohibit the exhibition of some animals. Displaying the bird of prey that you found at a flea market that had been sitting in someone's attic for twenty-five years may land you in jail and cost you

and the person from whom you bought it a significant fine. Know the rules in your state.

At the same time, antique deer heads, birds, fish and other taxidermy are available and can certainly be used. Also remember that almost all ungulates—moose, elk, deer and other two-toed animals—lose their antlers each year. Interestingly enough, the Boy Scouts in the Rocky Mountain states have exclusive rights to harvest elk antlers in Wyoming and Montana, and each year an auction is held of all antlers collected by the many scout troops, which make an effort to pick up as many antlers as possible. The antlers are sold by the pound to the highest bidder. The people who buy them make knife handles, chandeliers, floor lamps, and all sorts of other interesting items. Many of the other antlers are simply mounted and sold to decorators around the country for different projects.

Items made from antlers are collectible as well as decorative. Usually produced in Europe in the Black Forest region, Switzerland, Scotland and England, these articles are considered rare and very desirable. Treasures created from the antlers of fallow deer, caribou, elk, and other ungulates include clocks, pen-and-ink sets, picture frames, letter holders, racks, chafing dishes, candle stands, and gun and fishing-pole holders. Antlers have also been transformed into many types of lighting, including table lamps and chandeliers. In addition, major pieces of furniture were occasionally adorned with antlers, including desks and bookcases, arm and side chairs, umbrella stands, and numerous other antiques.

Be warned, however, that during the thirties, many people made look-alike antler items out of paper-mâché and other composite materials that can fool the average collector. Paper-maché antler articles break easily and are significantly lighter than real ones. Frequently seen paper-maché antler pieces include table mirrors, clocks, hair-brushing sets, and other rustic accessories. Paper-maché items are highly collectible but do not warrant the high prices that things made from real antlers command.

Although some people find it "a bit much," there were some very interesting articles made from deer and moose hooves from the turn of the century until the thirties. These items include lamps, hat and coatracks of all sizes and shapes, ashtrays, and more. They were produced by a number of companies that specialized in taxidermy and today are considered collectible.

ABOVE A contemporary bear is a great receptor for all sorts of small things and brings a sense of humor to the room. The bear was hand carved by Rick Turnbull.

PAINTINGS AND OTHER ARTWORK

Another way to bring nature indoors is through paintings and other artwork. The three most-common outdoor rustic pictures depict deer and elk, fish and creel, or a string of fish. One should usually be able to find any of these scenes at almost every flea market or antique show in the country, and they are inexpensive and look great in rustic rooms.

On the other hand, fine oil paintings can be very expensive. It is not uncommon for high-end artwork to command hundreds of thousands of dollars at auctions. That is not to say that really good art is not available to the average collector or decorator. There are plenty of quality rustic paintings showing log cabins, hunting and fishing moments, mountains and sunsets that can enhance the ambience of any rustic setting. Buy something you like, and make sure it's in excellent condition and comes

RIGHT The top half of a rowboat is creatively transformed into shelving in this Victorian country home. The painted pack basket and paddles add depth to the room.

with a written guarantee from the seller if he or she claims the artist is listed or otherwise well known.

It should also be mentioned that prints of many really great paintings that have outdoor themes are available to tenacious shoppers, including artwork by Frederic Remington, Winslow Homer, and many others. To work well in a rustic interior, these pictures should have clean matting and be set in frames that look old.

TEXTILES AND RUGS

Textiles can really add drama to a room. The right curtains, colorful upholstery and pillows, and warm rugs and blankets bring out the best in their settings. Indian rugs have always looked good almost anywhere. The bold geometric patterns and dramatic reds, grays, and browns of Navajo rugs can "jump-start" any room. Indian blankets and Beaver State shawls and robes made by Pendleton are great finishing touches. Wool blankets by firms such as Earlys and the Hudson Bay Company contribute prominent accents.

Other rugs used frequently in the rustic environment include Arts and Crafts wool and hemp rugs, kilims from Turkey, and dhurries in soft pastel colors. Hooked rugs depicting rustic scenes also look great hanging on walls or covering floors in low-traffic areas. The most desirable of the hooked rugs are the wonderful floor coverings made by Grenfell Industries in Canada. Motifs include outdoor scenes featuring geese, polar bears, and winter and fall backgrounds. Grenfell rugs are characterized by very tight stitching and are usually signed with a small label on the reverse side.

When buying antique rugs of any sort, get down on your hands and knees and smell them. Avoid rugs with animal scents. Check for moth holes and blood stains that may be impossible to get out. Reject carpets where the colors have run together. Most importantly, buy something you like; don't be talked into anything by an assertive salesperson. Only buy expensive floor coverings and other items from reputable dealers, and always get a written guarantee.

TWIG STANDS

Every beginning rustic collector in the world starts off with one of the ubiquitous three-legged twig stands that were made by the millions in every state in the Union. I can't count how many individuals have told me that they are the proud owner of a rare piece of rustic furniture, only to have it turn out to be a three-legged stand. Sometimes these stands were made with little ashtrays on top. Others had log cabins built onto the shelf or were decorated with gray and red paint. Some may have either a horseshoe or heart made of bent twigs adorning the side. A few of them have little chip carvings on many of the twigs, and only very rarely will you find a stand with a mosaic twig top. In any case, every collector should have at least one twig stand in his or her collection. They are cute and readily available.

WOODEN SOUVENIRS

Another category of items that are becoming popular are known as either "weird-wood" or "souvenir" wooden accessories. Generally these articles were made from ash trees and constructed into clocks, stands, wishing wells, tables, beer steins, ashtrays, nut bowls, cups and numerous other pieces of rusticana. Often they are adorned with decals of Indian chiefs or signed with the locale where they were bought. Exactly who produced these souvenirs is not known, but it is thought that thousands of them were made and sold to various tourist-trade markets. Collections of souvenir wooden items are easy to assemble and very affordable. One antique dealer showed up at a local flea market in Massachusetts

Every beginning rustic collector in the world starts off with one of the ubiquitous three-legged twig stands that were made by the millions in every state in the Union.

with over a thousand souvenir wooden articles and, surprisingly enough, sold them all to one collector.

BIRCHBARK ACCESSORIES

Birchbark items are also very desirable. Birchbark picture frames, lined with sweet grass and made by Indian craftspeople, look great on walls and tabletops. Birchbark canoes, containers, wastebaskets, mirrors, tepees, tie racks, mugs, place mats, bottle holders, and other pieces are wonderful items for collections.

INDIAN ARTIFACTS

Indian crafts of all kinds look great in rustic rooms. Baskets, artwork, textiles, rugs, dolls, beadwork and jewelry, and other objects made by Native Americans are both collectible and desirable. Several informative books that offer significant information on Indian artifacts are currently available. Review them before beginning a serious collection of Indian artwork, for the more you know about a subject, the better your collection will be. The finer pieces of Indian artwork are very expensive, and common sense dictates that we become informed consumers.

RUSTIC LIGHTING

Antique rustic lighting has always been very difficult to locate and use effectively. Occasionally, you

In short, rustic settings can be enhanced by all sorts of accessories.

may find rustic lamps made of rhododendron roots, birchbark, hickory branches, burls, twisted vines, logs of all shapes and sizes, and other organic materials. Interestingly enough, there seem to be many more intriguing rustic lamp shades than lamps. Look for shades made out of parchment, paper, or mica. Many of these feature impressive depictions of outdoor scenes and animals. Once again, if you locate and use antique lighting, make sure it has been rewired so you don't risk electrical fires.

In short, rustic settings can be enhanced by all sorts of accessories. Certainly don't limit yourself to the abbreviated list above. Try a variety of things, and if you don't like one, choose something else. Other old accessories that bring ambience into rustic settings are globes, lanterns, saws and lumberjack items, hunting jackets, weather vanes, leather-

bound books, outdoor magazines, Indian relics of all sorts, totem poles, croquet sets, picnic-basket sets, and numerous other articles that a little creativity can put together. Quite frankly, nothing is more fun than decorating your dream vacation lodge or cottage. Don't forget the plants and animals, because they are a significant part of nature. Get busy and go to it.

COLLECTING CONCERNS

Here are a few suggestions about purchasing items. One of the nice things about quality antiques is that, for the most part, they retain their value and often appreciate over the years. There are, however, a few very simple rules that will help ensure that your collection gains financially and aesthetically.

❧ Only buy things that are in excellent condition. Don't think that you are "getting a deal" just because something has a defect and is cheaper than an item in good condition. Remember the old adage that quality costs more. Avoid pieces that are broken.

❧ Try to buy pieces that have the original finish on them. Patina, the color that characterizes old pieces after time, is very important. Don't refinish something unless it absolutely needs it. Items that have old paint on them are considered very desirable. If you don't like the color of the paint, then don't buy the piece.

🌿 Buy things you really love. If you appreciate a certain item, chances are that someone else will feel the same way when you decide to part with it later.

🌿 Buy items that are functional. Certain chairs may look great, but if they are too rickety to use, their value is significantly less.

🌿 When examining an item for possible purchase, always ask the seller, "What has been done to the piece? Have there been any repairs? Is it old or new?" Get a guarantee in writing.

🌿 When buying at antique shows and flea markets, always arrive as early as possible. As a rule, all the "great buys" are gone within a half hour of a show opening. The early bird gets the outstanding antiques. Most shows have an "early buyer's" pass which costs a few dollars more than the general-admission price. I feel a little sorry for the retail buyers, knowing that the average antique changes hands four times between dealers before ever being offered to the public.

🌿 Find out who the reputable antique dealers are in your area and let them know what you are looking for and your price range.

🌿 Don't be afraid to negotiate a price with individuals who sell at antique markets. Usually most

A B O V E This Adirondack mirror is trimmed with twigs and was probably made at the turn of the century. The star is a traditional folk-art motif that is frequently utilized in rustic mosaic patterns.

dealers expect this and will alter their prices accordingly. However, be sensible; if something is marked $100, don't offer $10 for it. This will only insult the dealer and create ill will. Dealers deserve to make a living. If you can't offer at least 75 percent of the asking price, then don't offer at all. Also remember that people who pay cash always get a better price.

🌿 Be very careful at auctions. It's very easy to get carried away and spend significantly more money than you originally intended. A few years ago I attended an auction in western Massachusetts. In the auction was a wonderful root chair that

I knew I could sell for about $1,200, so I set my bidding limit at $950. In the heat and passion and bidding war of the auction, I eventually ended up paying $3,050 for the chair. I cursed myself all the way home for paying so much. But because the chair was a magnificent item and in excellent condition, I eventually sold it for a profit. However, I still think of the experience whenever I attend auctions and remind myself not to get carried away.

🌿 Another caution about auction items: sometimes dealers can't sell a particular piece, so it will be placed in an auction to "move it down the road." Did you ever wonder why most auction halls are so dark? Examine items very carefully prior to bidding at auction sales, and don't buy any junk.

🌿 Don't be afraid to work at building a great collection. It may take years to amass a significant collection because the really great pieces are rare and hard to come by. You will find that hunting the treasures can become obsessive. Many people find "chasing around after artworks" to be the most enjoyable thing in their lives. Almost all antique dealers actually start out this way.

BUYING, CARE AND OTHER CONCERNS

lthough rustic furniture looks

as if it belongs outside, in reality it cannot withstand

direct exposure to rain, snow and other natural

elements for extended periods. Rustic items are made of

wood, and, in time, all organic materials will decay, which

explains why so many pieces have been lost over the years.

Although it is true that many modern pieces may last several years outside, especially if they have been painted or chemically pressure treated with preservatives, nonetheless, antique rustic items made of wood should remain on covered porches or inside. They definitely should not be exposed to rain and moisture, since eventually decomposition will occur.

WHAT TO LOOK FOR WHEN BUYING

Often gray and weathered pieces turn up in the rafters of old garages and cellars, or at antique shows and flea markets. A usual first temptation is to purchase them before someone else does. However, several variables, such as the condition of the structure of the chair, the finish, the weaving on the seats, etc., should be considered before making a decision to purchase.

Because of the informal nature of rustic furniture, the majority of pieces have been subject to serious misuse and abuse. For instance, most chairs left on front porches have endured years of vacationers leaning back in them, placing great stress on the back legs. Don't buy chairs with broken back legs. Although many people will swear that the legs can be repaired by doweling them, experience shows that, sooner or later, the weakened legs

will break again. Best not to buy the chairs in the first place. The only effective way to remedy broken back legs is to completely replace the section where the break is. Unfortunately, because of the unusual curves in most chair legs, this is often difficult, if not impossible.

Other broken or missing parts can easily be replaced by cutting a heavy stick or branch from a local hardwood tree and coloring it to blend in with the rest of the chair. Make sure that the replacement part has been adequately dried prior to use. Logically, the part used in the repair, if possible, should be the same type of wood as the rest of the item.

All spindles or dowels in chairs or tables were originally secured with a nail driven in to lock them in place. These nails must be removed prior to replacement, and don't forget to add some good wood glue to the joint for extra security.

Before purchasing a chair or table, you should always check the height of the piece you are considering. Many items left outside have lost height. In other words, they have stood on moist ground so long that their feet have rotted away. The majority of chair seats stand between sixteen and eighteen inches off the ground; if they are lower than that, the chair may have lost height. Check the bottom of the feet for rot, and be aware that some-

ABOVE Rustic builders are all around the country. This builder in Washington State creatively uses native materials to fabricate an advertising sign.

one may have sawed off the bottom portion of the legs to make the chair sit level.

One way to check for height with Indiana hickory chairs and tables is to remember that these pieces originally had a slight bevel on the bottom of the legs. This was done at the factory to help prevent the bark from peeling as the pieces aged.

You should also check the bottom of the rockers on rocking chairs. Many times these chairs have sat for so long that the rockers have worn flat and, consequently, do not rock properly. Rockers are easily replaced. Don't forget to save the old rockers so that the person cutting the new ones can have a basic idea of the lengths and curves needed.

Another reason for the demise of rustic chair parts may be your

friendly neighborhood dog. A friend used to bring her golden retriever to my home for an afternoon of fun and play. His main hobby (and sole purpose in life) was fetching sticks. Needless to say, when left alone, he would attack one (unfortunately always the same one) of the many hickory chairs in my house. This dog got a big kick (no pun intended) out of chewing up my dining chair. Luckily, my neighbor finally decided to leave the dog at home during visits. Nevertheless, a good many chairs, tables, stools and other pieces made of sticks and branches bear scars or have met their downfall due to overly zealous canines; so be aware of your dog's behavior.

Check the chairs and tables very carefully for other signs of wood rot. Chairs that are still good

and solid should have significant weight to them. They should be very tight in construction and not wobbly or rickety.

Also check for insect infestation. Particularly look for small holes about the size of a pinhead. These holes mean that powder-post beetles have dined on the piece. A few holes are acceptable and treatable; too many holes and the chair should be avoided. If the chair has sat somewhere for a long period of time, check under it for small mounds of sawdust. If they are present, the piece should be removed and treated for insects immediately. Contact your local hardware store for sprayable insecticides. Also examine old chairs for bark lifting, which usually indicates that the chair is especially dry and in need of restoration.

RESTORING OLD CHAIRS

A gray and weathered chair can be restored readily, but not without effort. Several methods may be used. Orange shellac works wonders on an old gray finish but has a tendency to be glossy and uneven. Use it sparingly and experiment on a small section of the piece first.

You may also wish to bleach the wood and then varnish or polyurethane the chair with a flat or satin finish. Wood bleaches and

RIGHT Victorian antler chandelier, inside a lodge in the rain forest of Washington State.

similar products are available at hardware stores, or you may use simple household bleach. Whichever you choose, be sure to wash the wood thoroughly after bleaching it, since residual bleach will cause polyurethane and other finishes to streak and cloud.

Often, however, just a coat of varnish over the old finish is enough to revitalize a piece. Occasionally, just soap and water alone will perk up a worn item. You may also wish to try waxing the tops of tables or using plain furniture oil on the wood. A combination of boiled linseed oil and turpentine is the time-honored finish but may take some time to dry and could become "tacky" on humid days. Tung oil has also been used with excellent results to restore furniture.

REPAIRING SEATS

Usually the first parts that require repair on rustic furniture are the woven seats found on the majority of Indiana hickory pieces and many other chairs and settees. These chair seats are made of rat-

tan, wood splint, or other organic materials. In time, due to overuse and natural aging, the fibers will weaken and break. It is easy to replace these seats, and most people can do the job themselves. It should take no more than two hours to replace a seat, and with practice only about an hour. Many adult education classes offer courses in chair weaving and caning, or a local arts-and-crafts shop can give you the names of individuals who can show you how to do it. Several books are presently available that also demonstrate how it's done.

But don't hesitate to take on the job yourself; it's infinitely rewarding and really quite easy.

Once again, keep your furniture dry, oil it every year or so, and keep and eye out for insects.

REPRODUCTIONS

Anyone who attends the larger antique shows and flea markets around the country knows that every conceivable art form ever imagined by humankind is being reproduced today, and with good reason. First of all, "it's just good stuff, so why not," and in addition, the old stuff is next to impossible to find and very expensive when it is available.

The Amish still make wonderful twig items. Three companies in Indiana, as well as the prison system, are making hickory furniture. Western articles are once again being produced in Wyoming and antler chandeliers in Montana. Wonderful birch and twig items are coming out of the northern woods region. Furthermore, at last count, there were approximately five hundred individuals around the country creating all sorts of wild items out of twigs, sticks, antlers, driftwood, roots and every other organic material ever invented by the forces of nature.

There are several considerations for the consumer contemplat-

ABOVE A builder exhibits his crafts at the annual Rusitc Builders Show at the Adirondack Museum, Blue Mountain Lake, New York.

ing new items. With the exception of the work of very few makers, new things decrease in value, and old things increase. So the general underlying principle, whether you are dealing with new or old, is to buy quality. Find pieces that are really well made, that are aesthetically pleasing, that are sturdy, strong, and comfortable. Try out the chairs. Are they comfortable? Do they fit under the dining table? Are they well made? Do you trust the person who is selling them? Make sure that you really love the piece and are not buying it just because it's trendy.

Also, and this is very important, ask the person selling the item if it is old or new. I can assure you that many of the pieces being made today can fool even those who are accustomed to handling rustic

things every day, so be careful. And, equally as revealing, there are people out there who will sell you things that they will guarantee are old but which really were made just a few weeks before. As always, keep the items dry and out of direct sunlight, and immediately repair any damage that might occur.

Find pieces that are really well made, that are aesthetically pleasing, that are sturdy, strong, and comfortable.

CONTEMPORARY MAKERS AND SOURCES

If you're looking for rustic furniture, there are two choices: find antiques or buy new pieces. Antiques carry a certain mystique that makes them desirable, but there is a lot to be said for newly made furniture. One practical consideration is size. The majority of beds made during the early years were quite small and certainly do not meet the standard of king and queen sizes of today. Consequently, it is significantly easier to have beds and other items made rather than to spend years trying to locate certain antique items that are probably impossible to find anyway.

Another difficulty in finding antiques is that the early rustic makers produced only limited quantities of furniture. For instance, Earnest Stowe, often regarded as the premier North Woods builder of birch and twig furniture, is thought to have made around 125 pieces, many of which are in the Adirondack Museum in Blue Mountain Lake, New York. Consequently, it is impossible to collect his furniture.

There are about five hundred individuals, as well as several companies around the country, that are presently making rustic furniture. The makers are capable of producing anything imaginable out of just about any type of natural material available.

New rustic furniture can be found at many of the large annual outdoor flea markets and antique shows, including those held in Brimfield, Massachusetts; Kutztown, Pennsylvania; Atlanta, Georgia; Springfield, Ohio; and many others. Another suggestion is to pick up a copy of your regional antique newspaper and find out where and when the large antique markets are open.

If you really want to see some of the great makers from the East Coast, the Adirondack Museum in upstate New York has a yearly exhibit and sale for new rustic furniture makers. The show is held in the fall, and between twenty-five and fifty makers show their creations, take orders, and exchange ideas about trends in the business. The week prior to the show, the museum also sponsors an Adirondack Antique Show and sale on items from that region. Both weekends are excellent for a trip to the region, as the fall foliage is in full bloom and the Adirondack scenery is marvelous.

You may also wish to attend the annual Western Design Conference held in Cody, Wyoming. Not only are there lectures by experts on rustic furniture, but about twenty-five of the best western rustic builders exhibit their products.

Along with rustic furniture reproductions, a lot of new creations are surfacing. In fact, very few builders, unless directly requested to do so, are making exact copies of others' work. In reality, the majority of builders have their own vision of what rustic furniture should look like. They are influenced by what they see, but they also create their own art with natural materials.

Following are lists of sources for buying new and old rustic furniture and accessories.

GALLERIES

ABC Carpet
888 Broadway
New York, NY 10003
(212) 473-3000

Adirondack Store and Gallery
109 Saranac Ave.
Lake Placid, NY 12946
(518) 523-2646

Adirondack Trading Post
91 Main St.
Lake Placid, NY 12946
(518) 523-3651

Black Mountain Antique Mall
100 Sutton Ave.
Black Mountain, NC 28711
(704) 669-6218

Davis/Torres Antiques
410 Bonner
Bozeman, MT 59715
(406) 587-1587

Garden Living
206 Sutton
Black Mountain, NC 28711

Lake Placid Antique Center
103 Main St.
Lake Placid, NY 12946
(518) 523-3913

Newel Art Gallery
425 E. 53rd
New York, NY 10022
(212) 758-1970

Peter Roberts Gallery
134 Spring St.
New York, NY 10012
(212) 226-4777

Summer House in Highlands
Third at Spring St.
Highlands, NC 28741
(704) 526-9414

Whispering Pines
516 Main St.
Piermont, NY 10968

York Antique Gallery
Route 1, Box 303
York, ME 03909
(207) 363-5002

ANTIQUE DEALERS

Robert Burger
Box 02015
Columbus, OH 43202
(614) 262-9158

Linda Cassidy
Alpine Mall
Lake Placid, NY 12946
(518) 891-5873

Linda Davidson
296 Lakeshore Dr.
Berkeley Lake, GA 30136
(404) 448-2773

Bob Doyle
Box 565
Lake Placid, NY 12946
(518) 523-2101

Don Ellis
R.R. 3
DunDas, Ont. L9H 5E3, CANADA
(416) 648-1837

Harold Holmes
R.F.D. 3
Skowhegan, ME 04976
(207) 474-8769

Margot Johnson
18 E. 68th St., #1A
New York, NY 10021
(212) 794-2225

Ralph Kylloe
298 High Range Rd.
Londonderry, NH 03053
(603) 437-2920

Michael Meadows
919 Stiles St.
Baltimore, MD 21202
(410) 837-5427

Alan Pereske
Saranac Lake, NY 12983
(518) 891-3733

Ross Brothers (Boats and Canoes)
28 N. Maple St.
Florence, MA 01060
(413) 586-3875

Sioux Antiques
Box 24711
Omaha, NE 68124
(402) 391-8487

Cloanne Snyder
R.R. 4, Box 66
North Manchester, IN 46962
(219) 982-6608

INTERIOR DECORATORS

Barbara Collum
6976 Colonial Dr.
Fayetteville, NY 13066
(315) 446-4739

William Diamond Design
270 Lafayette St., Suite 1510
New York, NY 10012
(212) 966-8892

Mariette Gomez
241 E. 78 St.
New York, NY 10021
(212) 288-6956

Jed Johnson
211 W. 61 St.
New York, NY 10023
(212) 489-7840

Naomi Leff
12 W. 27 St.
New York, NY 10001
(212) 686-6300

Marjorie Shusman Inc.
15 W. 53 St., Apt. 35A
New York, NY 10019
(212) 975-1200

Dale Trice
1600 DeFoors Walk, NW
Atlanta, GA 30318
(404) 355-6667

MISSION AND ARTS AND CRAFTS DEALERS

Dennis Antiques
756 Park Ave.
Cranston, RI 02910
(401) 781-5694

Paul Fiori
P.O. Box 353
Cotuit, MA 02635
(508) 428-2415

Michael Fitzsimmons Gallery
309 W. Superior
Chicago, IL 60610
(312) 787-0496

Ray Groll
P.O. Box 421 Station A
Flushing, NY 11358
(718) 463-0059

JMW Gallery
144 Lincoln
Boston, MA 02111
(617) 338-9097

Mission Oak Shop / Market
Place Gallery
109 Main St.
Putnam, CT 06260
(203) 928-6662

David Rago
17 S. Main St.
Lambertville, NJ 08530
(609) 397-9377

Richard Gallery
2 Byrdcliffe
Woodstock, NY 12498
(914) 679-7561

ADIRONDACK BUILDERS

Barney Ballinger
P.O. Box 404B
Paradise Point
Mayfield, NY 12117

Glenn Bauer
32 McClelland St.
Saranac Lake, NY 12983
(518) 891-5104

The Bears Hand
R.D. 1, Box 111C
Schroon Lake, NY 12870
(518) 532-7636

Andy Brown
Hearthwoods of Michigan
P.O. Box 466
Lakeside, MI 49116
(616) 469-4220

Marvin Davis/Bob O'Leary
Romancing the Woods
33 Raycliffe Dr.
Woodstock, NY 12498
(914) 246-6976

Jay Dawson
R.D. 1, Box 257
Lake Clear, NY 12945
(518) 891-5075

Lillian Dodson
133 Crooked Hill Rd.
Huntington, NY 11743

Bill Duffy
281 Salt Springville Rd.
Ft. Plain, NY 13339
(518) 993-4422

Jerry Farrell
P.O. Box 255
Sidney Center, NY 13839
(607) 369-4916

Ron Fields
Shasta Six
400 N. Washington Dr.
Mt. Shasta, CA 96067
(916) 926-2091

Ruth and Charles Green
R.D. 1, Box 174
Ashville, NY 14710
(716) 763-9818

Brad Greenwood
13624 Idaho-Maryland Rd.
Nevada City, CA 95959
(916) 273-8183

Barry Gregson
Charlie Hill Rd.
Schroon Lake, NY 12870
(518) 532-3984

Dave Hall
P.O. Box 321
Bloomington, NY 12913
(518) 523-2697

Karl Hanck
Starbuck Rd.
P.O. Box 89
Fort Ann, NY 12827

Bobby Hansson
2068 Tome Highway
Port Deposit, MD 21904
(410) 658-3959

Bud Hanzlick
Bekan Rustic Furniture
P.O. Box 323
Belleville, KS 66935
(913) 527-2427

Timothy Hayes
R.R. 1, Box 168
Brattleboro, VT 05301
(802) 254-8448

Ken Heitz
Backwoods Furnishings
Box 161, Rt. 28
Indian Lake, NY 12842
(518) 251-3327

Steve Heller
Fabulous Treecraft Furniture
Rt. 28
Boiceville, NY 12412
(914) 657-6317

Andrew Himmen
75 Pequot Rd.
Southampton, MA 01073
(413) 538-8745

James E. Howard
P.O. Box 413
Long Lake, NY 12847
(518) 624-3813

Gib Jaques
Box 791
Keene Valley, NY 12943
(518) 576-9802

Stuart Johnstone
Wicopi Studios
P.O. Box 87
Chestertown, NY 12817
(518) 494-2171

Jackson Levi-Smith
Sagamore Conference Center
Raquette Lake, NY 13436
(315) 354-4303

Daniel Mack
Rustic Furnishings
3280 Broadway
New York, NY 10027
(212) 926-3880 or
(914) 986-7293

Lionel Maurier
26 Tucker Mountain Rd.
Meredith, NH 03253
(603) 279-4320

Brent McGregor
Box 1477
Sisters, OR 97759
(503) 549-1322

Glen A. Monson
Blue Mountain Woods
1025 N. 100 W.
Orem, UT 84057
(801) 224-1347

Tom Phillips
Star Rt. 2
Tupper Lake, NY 12986
(518) 359-9648

Will Pryor
Hawk Feather
R.D. 1, Box 117 A-1
Smyrna, NY 13464
(607) 336-3537

David Robinson
106 E. Delaware Ave.
Pennington, NJ 08534
(609) 737-8996

Abby Ruoff
Wood-Lot Farms
Star Rt. 1
Shady, NY 12479
(914) 679-8084

Ronald Sanborn
Hulls Falls Rd.
Keene, NY 12942
(518) 576-9593

Crispin Shakeshaft
R.R. 1, Box 25
Crown Point, NY 12928
(518) 597-3304

Dennis Smith
R.F.D. 3
Malone, NY 12953
(518) 483-8108

Peter Sparks
Waterfront Hoop Back
P.O. Box 4161
Burlington, VT 05406

Stickney Brook Furniture
R.R. 1, Box 168
Brattleboro, VT 05301
(802) 254-8448

Hutch Travers
Rt. 1, Box 230
Wake Forest, NC 27587
(919) 528-0458

David Vana
276 Averyville Rd.
Lake Placid, NY 12946
(518) 523-1899

Micki Voisard
999 Conn Valley Rd.
St. Helena, CA 94574
(707) 963-8364

Jack Waller
P.O. Box 453
Phillipsburg, MT 59858
(406) 859-3564

BENT TWIG BUILDERS

Greg Adams
914 E. Adams St.
Muncie, IN 47305
(317) 282-7158

Added Ooomph!
P.O. Box 6135
High Point, NC 27262
(919) 869-6379

The Amish Country Collection
P.O. Box 5085
New Castle, PA 16105
(412) 654-0919

Margaret Craven
14 12th Ave.
Longmont, CO 80501
(303) 772-1951

Gary Dannels
Beacon Woodcraft
307 Kilbourn
Beacon, IA 52534
(515) 673-6210

Davis and Wentz Hickory Furniture
New Paris, PA 15554
(814) 539-2691

Devonshire
P.O. Box 760
Middleburg, VA 22117
(703) 687-5990

Michael Emmons
Bare Bones
Partington Ridge
Big Sur, CA 93920
(408) 667-2133

Faircloth and Croker
Highway 11 South, Box 263
Rising Fawn, GA 30738
(706) 398-2756

Liz Sifrit Hunt
Box 218176
Columbus, OH 43221
(614) 459-1551

Richard and Lisa Ianni
A-Ya Art
P.O. Box 23
St. Johnsville, NY 13452
(518) 568-5015

La Lune Collection
930 E. Burleigh
Milwaukee, WI 53212
(414) 263-5300

A. C. Latshaw
Rustic Furniture
New Paris, PA 15554
(814) 733-4640

Laughing Willows
Partington Ridge
Big Sur, CA 93920
(408) 667-2133

Masterworks
P.O. Box M
Marietta, GA 30061
(404) 423-9000

James McGee
P.O. Box 645
Spring City, TN 37381

Clifford Monteith
Twiggery
P.O. Box 9
Lake Ann, MI 49650
(616) 275-6560

Paula Moody and Barry Jones
Tiger Mountain Woodworks
Box 28
Tiger Mountain, GA 30576
(404) 782-7286

Phillip and Kathy Payne
Rt. 3, Box 1020
Broadhead, KY 40409
(606) 758-8587

Pure and Simple
117 W. Hempstead
P.O. Box 535
Nashville, AR 71852

E. N. Raber
Pope Rd.
Randolph, NY 14772

Peggy Yoder
Hickory Rockers of Berlin
Box 235
Berlin, OH 44610
(216) 893-2680

WESTERN FURNITURE MAKERS

Philip Clausen
Rt. 1, Box 3397
Coquille, OR 97432

Jack Favour
1300 Middlebrook Rd.
Prescott, AZ 86303
(602) 445-0698

Great American Log
Furniture Company
P.O. Box 3360
Ketchum, ID 83340
(800) 624-5779

Jake Lemon
P.O. Box 2404
Sun Valley, ID 83353
(208) 788-3004

Lodgepole Manufacturing
Star Rt. 15
Jackson, WY 83001
(307) 733-3199

Matt Madsen
Burl Art Productions
P.O. Box 187
Orick, CA 95555
(707) 488-3795

Susan Parish
2898 Glascock
Oakland, CA 94601
(510) 261-0353

J. Mike Patrick
New West Furniture
2119 Southfork
Cody, WY 82414
(307) 587-2839

John and Gary Phillips
The Drawknife
P.O. Box 280
Driggs, ID 83422
(208) 456-2560

Rick Turnbull
Box 3814
Breckenridge, CO 80424

Judd Weisberg
Rt. 42
Lexington, NY 12452
(518) 989-6583

John Feyes
Willsboro Wood Products
P.O. Box 509
Keseville, NY 12944
(518) 834-5200

INDIANA HICKORY FURNITURE MAKERS

Flat Rock Furniture
R.R. 1, Box 403 A
Flat Rock, IN 47234
(812) 587-5871

Old Hickory
403 S. Noble St.
Shelbyville, IN 46176
(800) 232-2275

Tiger Mountain Woodworks
Box 249, Hwy. 106
Scaly Mountain, NC 28775
(704) 526-5577

ANTLER LIGHTING AND FURNITURE BUILDERS

Roc Corbet
P.O. Box 53
Charlo, MT 59824
(406) 644-2445

Gail Flynn Antler Artwork
3927 Oberlin Ct.
Tucker, GA 30084
(404) 491-0929

Ragged Mountain Antler
Chandeliers
106 Meadow Ln.
Marble, CO 81623
(800) 963-0708

BIBLIOGRAPHY

Flood, Elizabeth Clair. *Cowboy High Style: Thomas Molesworth to the New West.* Gibbs Smith, Publisher, Salt Lake City, Utah, 1992. This new book provides the reader with an in-depth look at western designer Thomas Molesworth and provides many photographs showing antique and contemporary western rustic furniture and contemporary makers.

Gilborn, Craig. *Adirondack Furniture.* Abrams, Publisher, New York, 1987. This book provides the details of Adirondack furniture and shows numerous examples.

Kylloe, Ralph. *The Collected Works of Indiana Hickory Furniture Makers.* Available from the author, 1990. The book provides an extended history of Indiana hickory furniture and shows more than 650 hickory items.

Mack, Dan. *Making Rustic Furniture.* Sterling Publishing Company, 1992. Presently the best book available on building rustic furniture. A short section of the history of rustic furniture is included. Many photos show different styles that are available today.

Osborne, Sue. *American Rustic Furniture.* Harmony Books, New York, 1984. Osborne provides the reader with a history of rustic furniture and shows through photographs the various styles that have evolved through the years.

Stephenson, Sue. *Rustic Furniture.* Nostrand Reinhold, Publisher, New York, 1979. This book provides an academic approach to the literature on the history of rustic furnishings. The book also reviews rustic furniture, mostly southern, in America.